DICK GREGORY

WAKE UP AND STAY WOKE: RUNNING FOR LIFE

DICK GREGORY
WAKE UP AND STAY WOKE: RUNNING FOR LIFE

DR. E. FAYE WILLIAMS, ESQ.

Noahs Ark Publishing Service
Beverly Hills, California

Dick Gregory Wake Up and Stay Woke: Running for Life

ISBN 978-1-7357447-2-8

Copyright © 2021 by E. Faye Williams

Published by:

Noahs Ark Publishing Service

8549 Wilshire Blvd., Suite 1442
Beverly Hills, CA 90211

www.noahsarkpublishing.com

Creative Contribution: Laval W. Belle
Editor: Carolyn Billups
Graphic Design: Christopher C. White
Interior Design: James Sparkman

Cover Photo (Dick Gregory at Southern Illinois University 1953-1954): Southern Illinois University Carbondale photograph collection, Special Collections Research Center, Southern Illinois University Carbondale.

This book is dedicated to all the people who gave me their Dick Gregory stories.

I also dedicate this book to my mother, Mrs. Frances LaCour Williams-Johnson.

CONTENTS

SERVICE AND FRIENDSHIP

At a young age, my father explained to me that I was born with all of the wisdom I would ever need. Navigating life takes tools. Most of the tools are mental and spiritual, yet they require crafting and refining. A healthy mind and body are not a given. We must work to offset infirmity. Eat to live. Garbage in equals garbage out; this includes the garbage we allow into our minds. There is nothing new under the sun, it's repackaged and rebranded. The 'isms' may have different names, but it's more of the same. It's a challenging world, so slow down and pace yourself. Realize that love gives us wings. Look out for the marginalized. In the end, what matters is the service we have provided to uplift humanity.

Keep it simple. Today's secrets were once common knowledge. Our armchair educations have reduced our innate intelligence. Our obsession with IQ has deteriorated our EQ. Good sense stopped being common long ago. Find your pathway back to nature. Harness natural hygienic factors: clean air, clean water, sunshine, moonlight, ocean waves, tall blowing grass, autumn foliage, blowing leaves and earth between our toes. Laughter, honesty, fairness and equality. Truth and reconciliation with the environment, respect given and respect received.

All the activity of a man/woman during his lifetime is lost in the grander scheme of things and will soon be forgotten.

Ecclesiastes 1:11

The universal elements: Earth, Fire, Water, Air, and Space from prehistoric times are the same elements that provide for life today. Commit to clean and sustainable living—a commitment to leaving the earth in better shape than we found it. If we knew better, we'd do better. Each one teach one. The power of one is amplified with like minds. Close your eyes, get grounded with the earth, feel the sun's warmth, breathe in the fresh air, feel the raindrops on your face, and allow your mind to wander off into the infinite ether where dreams direct calibrated decisions and those decisions bring about desired reality.

We have a big job. We have an important job. Have fun, but have fun quick because recess is just about over. My father would say that often. Since my father's death, I've had time to reflect on the things he'd say. I realized he was always preparing us in his unique way for what was next. "Give, Love, Serve" sums up how he lived his life.

My father died on August 19th, 2017 at 8:40 p.m. at a beautiful, boutique hospital on the outskirts of Northwest Washington, D.C. In his final hour, I found myself alone, standing guard at his operating room door, as four of the finest surgeons I've ever interacted with approached me with a blitzkrieg of difficult choices. The sounds of hard work and dutiful lifesaving were heard all around us. An additional team of doctors and nurses tended to my father just behind me. They were working hurriedly, yet not panicking. They were fighting to save a life, my father's life. It was surreal. With the insanity of the situation, I cracked the tiniest smile when I heard my dad's voice in my head, *"This is bullshit. Ain't no way all these white folks are doing all this to save a Black man's life."*

The effort was overwhelming. Teams worked to stabilize my father for a life support transport to George Washington University Hospital where a complicated and rarely successful surgery was planned. The odds of my father surviving transport alone were very slim. As his team discussed strategies, their faces were drained of color as they heard beeps, chirps, and codes that were familiar to them and indicated the fight was coming to an end. One nurse gave me the smallest head shake and then a nod. She didn't need to say any more. It indicated to me it was time to go be with my father.

My father knew we were not leaving that hospital. I held him tightly, standing to the left of his bed, my right arm firmly but gently gripping his forearm and my left hand gripping his thigh. My father was always the world's smallest yet biggest giant to me. He was 5'10" and weighed 140 pounds, but as anyone who experienced him could attest to, he might as well have been three times that size. He was always Herculean to me and to so many others. My father was in no pain and appeared very clear as to what was taking place. I took a few deep breaths because it seemed like I was forgetting to breathe. I am no preacher, but I knew the moment called for an exchange of words to complement the hands-on, tactile love we were exchanging. On the third breath, I bent over and loudly spoke directly into my father's left ear.

"Everything is absolutely okay, Pop. You are an amazing human being. I love and appreciate you beyond words. Breathe, relax, you can close your eyes. Your true work has only just begun. I love you and I will take care of everything and everybody. You make me incredibly proud!"

With that, I lifted back up, still holding on to my father for dear life. The thoughts racing through my mind at that moment were too numerous to account. He rolled or tilted his head to the left, flashed that textbook smile we've seen thousands of times as he graced stages around the world and with his left eye, he winked. It was the most beautiful facial expression I had ever seen. The wink pierced right to my core.

The doctor quickly brought back my mother, my siblings, my father's nephew, and two of my father's lifelong dear friends, Dr. E. Faye Williams and John Bellamy, to say their farewells. We stayed for hours crying, talking, laughing, and telling Pop stories. Members of the hospital rotated through to offer their condolences. They deal with death daily; however, they acknowledged that this loss felt different. Family, friends, and healthcare providers connecting with the universe, filled with sadness and joy for a life incredibly well-lived.

In the heaviness of this moment, I could see and feel so much lighthearted beauty. Oddly enough, I felt a strange but calming spirit as I recognized my father had lived a beautiful life cycle. He peacefully transitioned at the chronological age of eighty-four, surrounded by people who loved and adored him. This reality was not afforded to many of his friends—Martin, Medgar, and Malcolm were tragically denied their right to grow old with their friends and family. Ms. Cicely Tyson would always say, *"Once an adult, twice a child,"* and I was determined my father's second childhood would be filled with the joy and respect his first childhood was devoid of. For me, it is far more important how my father lived his life than how he died.

My father was born in 1932 on the 12th of October. It was a profoundly difficult time for a multitude of reasons. The roaring '20s were not so roaring for everyone. At the close of the decade, ominous times were ahead. August 1929 was the beginning of the Great Depression. My father just so happened to be born when America was at its absolute economic bottom. True misery ruled the day. October 1932 was the poorest month of the poorest year in America's history.

A black boy born in the 'Ville,' a section of St. Louis almost forgotten in time, a section where folks were marginalized solely for being black then re-marginalized for being poor. Poor and black, or black and poor, any way you looked at it the reality was tough. Jim Crow added insult to injury. No rights, no food, no clothes, but also no shame. As my father famously said, he had to go to school to learn that.

Throughout his life, my father had amazing friendships, friends willing to stand shoulder-to-shoulder in good times and bad. Superheroes many times work in teams. Folks can collaborate without friendship; however, collaborating with a true friend is where the magic happens.

Of all of the relationships in life, it is friendship that is so incredibly special—true friendships: real, organic and genuine. Friendship is not held together by contractual bonds or by bloodlines; it's a conscious decision to enter into or exit these relationships.

The life of an activist is difficult. There's no sick leave, no health insurance, no retirement plan. Just service for your people, a people who may or may not express gratitude. When your passion is pure, accolades mean very little. Driven by morals and

service, the battlefield of activism is safer with a teammate, friends
to peacefully cover their six. It's marvelous when your teammate
is also your best friend.

E. Faye Williams and Dick Gregory proved activists are born
not made. They crisscrossed the globe fighting for the underserved. This was and is their retirement plan. Activism is in their
DNA. A midday walk could, at the snap of a finger, transition
into a peaceful protest. They were both fixtures in Washington,
D.C.'s civil disobedience scene. The added benefit of E. Faye's
day job was when the going got tough and my father needed an
attorney, E. Faye would put on her lawyer hat and represent her
favorite client. Not all superheroes wear capes, but in my world,
they certainly carried signs and always kept a comfortable pair of
marching shoes nearby. I'm eternally grateful for E. Faye's famil-
ial friendship, but most grateful for the amazing friend she was
to my father. Give, Love, Serve. Thanks to friends like these the
world is certainly a better place.

In eternal friendship,
Dr. Christian Gregory

ACKNOWLEDGEMENTS

I would like to thank everyone who encouraged me to put my thoughts on paper because they thought this book would be therapeutic through my difficult days after my best friend, Dick Gregory, died.

I want to thank my publisher, Laval Belle, who pushed me to get started and who was there to lead me through the steps of getting this book done.

My thanks go to the staff at Noahs Ark Publishing who helped me with collecting the required permissions for use in this book.

I am grateful for Dr. Christian Gregory who read my ramblings and helped me to recall fine details that escaped my memory as I was writing.

I am grateful for Terrence Scott who assisted me with a lot of my responsibilities so as to give me the time and space to write.

Finally, I want to thank Katea Stitt, Program Director at WPFW 89.3 FM Radio, who gave me the opportunity to host a program in remembrance of Dick Gregory where listeners made me realize just how important Mr. Gregory was in not only my life but in the lives of many others.

INTRODUCTION

I met Dick Gregory (Greg) in 1986 when I ran for the U.S. Congress in Louisiana, my home state. After having so many people ask me for money before they came to support me, I was pleasantly surprised when he came to speak at a banquet for me and asked for nothing. After the campaign, I moved to Washington, D.C. where we met again. He began inviting friends to my home so he could cook meatless burgers for them and show them that everything in a burger was about the seasonings used! We used many different things to replace meat, such as black beans and eggplant. I became a believer and never again ate a piece of beef to this day!

At the time Dick Gregory passed away in 2017, we had been running buddies and best friends for over thirty years. We had run and walked together through rain, cold, snow, and heat at all times of the day. It was mostly before daylight in the morning when he was not on the road for shows or speaking engagements. His walking pace was like another person's running pace and I had a hard time keeping up with him at first. Ultimately, I learned to speed up my pace and I could keep up with him. We would walk for miles.

Often on weekends, we went in search of books, newspapers, and health equipment that one of us had heard about or read about and we looked for an endless number of vitamins and health supplements. He always carried his vitamins and water in his backpack, as well as numerous books, papers, and the latest gadget he had found or been given by someone. Somebody was always showing him some device and people gave him so many things. They thought if he approved of whatever it was, that was a great promotion. When visiting the first Tesla store in Washington, D.C., we received a very pleasant welcome and a complete talk and demonstration about the car. We had a chance to sit in the car while everything about it was being explained to us. At that time, I was not ready for a driverless car! I have since ridden in one with his son, Dr. Christian Gregory—and I am still not quite ready for one, but I do like Christian's car!

Greg and I would search for the best tennis walking shoes, the best beds, the best exercise equipment, the best eating places, and more. He loved movies and we saw so many. He'd often go back to see the same movies many times. Sometimes, it was to make sure friends saw them if he thought there were important messages in the movies. I came to believe the real reason was that he had to see them more than once to know what the movies were really about because many times, he was sleeping in the theater about five minutes into the movie and I wasn't always sure I understood the parts of the movie he'd slept through! I would keep nudging him to wake him up, and he would wake up for a while but waking him up was a losing battle because he went right back to sleep! He did that whenever he sat still for a few minutes. So, he saw different parts that he later put together to be able to really know what the movie was about! When he was excited about the message in a movie, he told everybody about it, and he often took them to see the movie.

There is still great interest in everything about Dick Gregory. So, one day I just decided to do this book so that people who didn't know him so well would learn what the real Dick Gregory was like when he wasn't on stage. He was so much more than his comedy and so much more than his fiery speeches. He has always been about social activism that made a positive difference in the lives of so many who often could or would not speak for themselves. Yes, a big part of his life was about comedy, but it was about so much more! No matter what happened in his life, he never viewed it through the rearview mirror. He was always forward looking, and he taught me to do that. That's why I was so blessed to know him and to be able to spend so much time with him.

CHAPTER 1

HOW I MET DICK GREGORY

I had previously heard of the great Dick Gregory, but I didn't actually meet him in person until I ran for the United States Congress in 1986 in Louisiana. He was in Louisiana visiting his daughter, Michelle, who was a student at Louisiana State University at the same time I had a campaign event in Baton Rouge. Congressman Mervyn Dymally of California came down to Louisiana on my behalf. He was my biggest supporter in the race, and he spoke with Greg and invited him to my event that evening. Greg came and so did Coach Dale Brown from LSU. (He and Greg were friends and remained so for the balance of Greg's life. Dale was one of the last people to call Greg the day he left us.) After my speech Greg spoke, or should I say he critiqued me, about all the lines I used that began with the words, *"My Mother taught me..."* He just made his jokes up on the spot and the crowd loved it. He said he didn't understand how I could remember so many things my Mother taught me when the only way he could get his children's attention was to pull a chair up and sit in front of the refrigerator. He said that is how you are sure to get their attention because the time always comes when they want something to eat. Without asking for a dime for any expenses, he was there and was supportive of whatever I was involved in since that time.

Rev. Jesse Jackson at a rally in support of Dr. E. Faye Williams during her run for U.S. Congress in 1986.

Congressman Dymally and Greg were friends and were there to support me when most of Louisiana's so-called VIPs would not come out in support of my campaign. The exception was Congressman Billy Tauzin. He was at my big event in Baton Rouge. Congressman John Breaux would come to my events from time to time because my crowds were often bigger than his; however, he never bothered to lend any support to me even though my campaign brought out a lot of votes for him. Governor Edwin Edwards was supportive in many ways. I was invited to events at the governor's mansion. I was welcome to stop by the mansion for lunch whenever I was in Baton Rouge. One newspaper reporter once saw Edwin and me talking at a public event and we were having such fun that the reporter could not resist writing an entire article questioning what we could possibly be talking about—and I will never tell! The late A.Z. Young, who worked for the governor and was a former member of the famous *Deacons for Defense of Bogalusa, Louisiana*, was very supportive.

I will always remember Representative Raymond Jetson, Attorney Marion White, Ulysses Addison, Corinne Maybuce, most of the St. James, St. John, Ascension Parish Black leaders and a few others who were there for me from the beginning of my campaign and never wavered.

When my campaign was over, some who had not supported me admitted they were shocked that I received so many votes. They finally admitted when it was too late that I could have won with a bit of help from more Black leaders, especially Black elected officials. I wound up winning over all of the Primary competition, coming in first in a crowd of five white males. I ran my race with little money. My first donation came from Congressman Dymally who, at the time, was my best friend. In the runoff, I won nearly 97,000 votes, something almost no candidates in the country needed in order to win. That is something no one else had done in those days in my state. Certainly, no Black person had done so in a Congressional race in Louisiana. Early in the evening I was announced as the projected winner. I even received congratulatory calls from around the country.

Unfortunately, the runoff results were called back and it was determined that I had lost by about sixth tenths of one percent! The tragedy was that more than 30,000 registered Black people in Baton Rouge alone had not voted. Just a reasonable amount of that vote would have been enough to overcome the approximately 5,000 votes by which the record shows I lost. So much for that! I moved back to Washington, D.C. where I had recently graduated from the Howard University School of Law and went to work on the staff of Congressman Dymally. I remained there until he retired. I did run again but the results were about the same. It seems that a majority of white Democratic leaders in the state had decided no matter how many votes I received, they'd prefer to have a white racist Republican. The state Democratic party chair gave me no help. Ultimately, it became clear to me that no matter how many votes I received, I would not be allowed to get credit for winning.

I never fail to thank the nearly 97,000 people who voted for me on my first time running for public office. Many still refer to me as "Louisiana's Congresswoman in Exile." That was a title first started by the Rev. Jesse Jackson and it was often used whenever I spoke publicly or was introduced in meetings. Rev. Jackson, along with Congressmen Bill Gray, Ed Towns, Ron Dellums, Charlie Hayes and others did campaign for me. As a matter of fact, all Congressional Black Caucus members actively supported me in some way, except Congresswoman Maxine Waters and I never asked her why.

I so much appreciate the elderly Black women who spoke up for their pastors to recognize me when I visited their churches. They often rose from their seats when the pastor chose not to recognize me as they had often done for other candidates. Some politely said to their pastor that I was there, and it would be a good idea to pick up a collection for me! We knew some of them were already in the pockets of my opponents because they forgot to conceal the checks in their shirt pockets when they met with me. I told them up front I was going to reveal it if they asked me for money to gain their support. I guess they believed me because none of them ever actually asked! I believe most of them did vote for me even if they could not actively support me.

I still remember many of my supporters and I hear from some of them from time to time. They call when a friend or relative dies to ask if I would write a message for the funeral program. Some of their adult children stay in touch and keep me informed of what is going on in their communities. Some still invite me to speak for events in their communities. Many who were too young to vote when I ran for office have grown up and run for office. Some are mayors of cities and on city councils and tell me I inspired them to run. Greg visited several of the towns where I had supporters. During those times, I would graciously take a back seat to him, but the people always thanked me for getting him there. He never said no to my requests when his calendar was open.

When I returned to Washington, where I had lived since law school, I gave myself six weeks to get over the loss. I still put limits on how long I will grieve over anything and work to meet that deadline. Congressman Dymally arranged a stay for me in Florida with Greg and his team at his Ft. Walton Beach Health Club. I had a chance to get to know Greg a bit better, but there was little time to just sit and talk with him. We were usually in a group setting listening to his lectures or walking on the beach and sometimes exercising. There were several staff members who worked with us that I later came to know well. Greg came in after we'd heard from the staff and all of us hung onto his every word. With the fresh air, the wading in the ocean, the long walks, the great company, and the healthy food, I recovered from the grueling Congressional campaign in record time.

I almost always called him Mr. Gregory. With all of the important sacrifices he made during the Civil Rights Movement

and beyond, it just never seemed right to refer to him as Dick—
something almost everyone else does, and always did.

After my return to Washington, I received a call from Greg
after he had concluded a show in Baltimore. He informed me that
he was stranded and asked if I would come to Baltimore to pick
him up so he could return to his residence in Washington, D.C.
Baltimore, not counting heavy traffic times, is almost an hour from
Washington. As much as I don't like driving at night, he charmed
me into going to Baltimore to pick him up. All the way there, I was
thinking, *"He really doesn't know me that well. Didn't he have anybody
else who could have picked him up?"* I did because of my great respect
for all of his civil rights work.

Greg really didn't know how I felt about people who were not
ready on time and how much I hated it when people who didn't
know how unhappy I was when anybody showed a lack of respect
for my time. Naturally, he wasn't ready when I arrived, so I had
to park and wait for him. At any rate, no matter how long I had
to wait, I really couldn't get angry with him. I had heard him talk
enough about how anger hurts the person who gets angry, not the
person to whom the anger is directed.

All the years I knew Greg, he marched to his own drumbeat
and he hurried for nothing or for no one! If you have ever traveled
with him, you know that he traveled very heavily and while in his
hotel room, he pulled out every book, every newspaper, every
vitamin and anything else he had packed to take along with him.
So, he had to figure out how to repack everything he brought
with him, including everything he acquired while there. That was
already a lot! I don't remember how long I had to wait for him to
get ready to leave the hotel, but I know it was late into the night.
I also learned that on time to him meant whenever he got ready!

So, I had to adjust. Naturally, whenever I picked him up, he was never ready by my time when I arrived, so I had to just park and wait for him many times. On the other hand, I was always ready when he picked me up.

A lot of people have called Greg their friend or their *good* friend, but those who know both of us knew that we were *best friends* and that's different from being just ordinary friends. His family was like my family and mine like his. He and Lillian had ten living children. The Gregory family has seven girls and three boys. My family has nine children. We have seven girls and two boys. We knew each other's family. Greg and my brother, Sonny, were great buddies. Both are gone now. He knew my brothers, sisters, nieces and nephews, and my mother. I know his spouse, one of his brothers, his children and many of his grandchildren.

I was invited to all of the Gregory special occasions nearby (birthdays, grandchildren's and children's programs, musicals, plays, etc.) and I made it a priority to be present whether he was in town or not. I have been on programs alongside his grandson, Busayo, a brilliant young man. He and I once served on a panel in observance of Dr. Martin Luther King, Jr. Day at a church in Maryland. Once we were finished with our presentations, he high fived me and said, *"You and I were the best."* I think he was right! He sounded just like his grandfather!

Mrs. Lillian Gregory (known to all and preferred to be called "Lil") often thanked me for the things I did for her family, and I hope she knows how helpful some members of her family have been for me and some still are. She has graciously thanked me for my help with her family while Greg was still with us, as well as since he has been gone. I have assisted with his health care a few times, most notably when he was a patient at Howard University

Hospital, and again when he spent his last week alive at Sibley Hospital in Washington, D.C. I have assisted with her birthday celebrations as well as Greg's.

Some members of Lil's family have done a lot for me, too, just by allowing me to have access to so much of his time to support our various causes, some mine, some his, some were mutual. I owe Lil a lot for the massive amount of time and talent their son, Dr. Christian Gregory, and I have shared. Christian is so kind, so smart that he has been a lifesaver for me since his Dad has been gone, as well as during the last year of his Dad's life. Sometimes, he works out of my office and spends many days at my place fixing one thing or the other. He supervised massive renovations to my office and my home. I am not sure what I would do without him. He joins several young men in my life that I call "my sons" or "my nephews." I am so blessed to have so many young people around who help me with various things.

Like so many Black people, including me, Greg grew up in poverty and had every reason to grow up hating a lot of things and people around him, but that isn't the way he was. While he could easily point out the negatives in the world, he always returned to love as being the answer and being the best way to solve problems. If someone around him began saying something negative, he would caution us by saying, *"Don't put it out there."* He believed that verbalizing the negative blocked the good that likely would happen otherwise.

Greg was born October 12th, 1932 in St. Louis, Missouri. He often told me about growing up and what a great challenge it was to have his wayward dad occasionally visit the home where his mom, brothers, and sisters lived. Those were not pleasant visits for him. I could relate to the situation because my dad left home when I was only eleven years old, and I remember the not too happy visits he sometimes made to our home. Greg talked with sadness how his dad, Presley (or "Big Prez" as he was known), would come to their home, expecting to discipline the kids, especially him, and leave behind his mother who became pregnant again. It was always sad to hear Greg even mention his dad who beat his mother savagely and beat him, too. He said he always resisted his father's attempts to discipline him, mainly because he didn't like the way he treated his mother and took the liberty to drop by at will and try to act like he had a right to be in charge. Greg paid a price for standing up to his dad and defiantly refused to cry when his father beat him.

In the early years of my life, I witnessed domestic violence with my parents, but unlike Greg's mother, my mother either escaped as we blocked my dad from getting to her or she fought back. My dad was over six feet tall. My mom was barely five feet, but she was fearless. Much later in life, when many of my family members were present, my father at least apologized for his behavior toward my mother. He blamed it on men in his day who thought that's what men were supposed to do! I have since worked against domestic violence for more reasons than one. I have helped many women who experienced domestic violence. I am a survivor of domestic violence. I have a lip that is stitched together, a wound on my abdomen that ultimately healed and a gunshot scar on one shoulder. For years, I looked over my shoulder when I was out and was uncomfortable being in the room with any male who was not related to me or that I had not known for a very long time. Greg always supported me in my work against domestic violence and any other problems I worked on for the benefit of women. We could spend hours talking about our early lives, both comparing and contrasting. He was in awe of all of the studying I had done and often bragged about it when introducing me to his friends.

I was aware of the way Greg grew up, and he was aware of how I grew up. We both had limited resources and in both our households there was domestic violence. Both things heavily impacted our lives and made for many discussions. We knew each other's background well and that had a lot to do with the kinds of projects and issues in which we were involved. He told me about his challenges in school where he was frequently embarrassed by certain teachers and while that never happened to me, I could relate to it from other students who were treated the same way. Early in life, I attended a one-room schoolhouse and later a two-room school. I knew the schools were inadequate and I had to pass by white schools to get to them. We had several grades taught by the same teacher who had to share her time with different grades.

As a 7th grader that was easy to see when I was called on to assist the teacher by leaving my class to work with the lower grades. After my 7th grade year, I had to attend a different school and the principal moved me almost immediately to 9th grade, which meant that I skipped 8th grade totally. I always assumed I missed something in 8th grade that I needed later in life. Nevertheless, the principal moved me to a higher grade where I was two years younger than my classmates, but he thought I could compete at the higher level. The only problem I had with the promotion before my entire class was moved up was that I had fallen in love (If 8th graders can fall in love or even know what love is!) with a classmate by the name of Dave Jones. I had to leave him behind to move to 9th grade that was held in a different part of the campus. Fortunately, he survived 8th grade without me, and we were reunited when he graduated to 9th grade and was one of the star basketball players. I became the secretary to the team and later played basketball so I could travel with the team. Unfortunately, that lasted for a short time when Mother decided to move us to another city about forty miles away, and I had to leave my first love again to attend another school.

Greg was lucky because initially he had a chance to remain in the same city as his first love, a little girl by the name of Helene. He lost her when his teacher humiliated him in class after he kept raising his little hand to report on what he would donate to the teacher's fundraiser. He wanted to impress Helene. The teacher refused to recognize his hand and when he persisted at being recognized, she told him to put his hand down by pointing out that he didn't even have a daddy. She said, in front of the class, that he was too poor to participate in donations to the school like Helene's father and how fathers of the other students did. I wanted to cry every time he told me that story. After all these years, I could tell he was still affected by that. Greg said he ran out of the classroom because he was too embarrassed and too humiliated to face Helene again! We shared our first heartbreaks about the pain we experienced losing our first love! I was moved to tears with his story. Eventually, I got over my love for my middle school's first crush and found a new love in my new high school when my mother moved. His name was Abe Brackins, and he was captain of the football team! The next love for Greg that I heard about was Lil and she remained so for the rest of his life!

As for me, I haven't been so blessed as to find the male version of Lil. Before Greg passed away, he often told me he wished I would find someone because he thought that I should be married. Why? I don't know, but I was never able to grant him that wish! At any rate, I know he would have behaved just like a typical father and would have found no one I presented for his inspection to be the right one!

I grew up in places where few of the women were married. Many had been married but had husbands who were dead or had moved on to other lives with other women, so it was left to our mothers to take care of us. In our family, there were nine children. I was born on a farm in Louisiana's most famous parish (known as counties outside the state) where we did sharecropping. The parish was Natchitoches, which most people generally do not know how to pronounce! Unlike Greg, I didn't know a lot about my family's history, but I later learned that a great (with too many greats to describe) grandmother had come to the little town of Melrose, in which I grew up, from Togo in French West Africa. I never learned who her husband was. My grandfather came from France. That's my mother's side of the family. Her father deserted her mother and, pretending he was dead, went to New Orleans and raised another family of several children which I learned about through an ancestry search in recent years. Since my mother was ninety-eight years old when I learned that, I chose not to tell her.

As for the rest of my mother's side of the family, we picked up our Native American blood from her mother. My father's side is a bit more complicated. His mother was Native American and White. I find my African blood from my father's father whose name was Ledgis Williams. That's what slavery did for our families. We can't be certain as to all of our blood. I have a little niece who explains that her mother is Mexican (she is). She says her father is Hispanic (he's not) and she says she is Black (she is). When asked how that happened, she just throws up her hands indicating she doesn't know. That's the explanation many of us in Louisiana have, trying to explain how all of our generations wound up Black. Nevertheless, we tell the world we are Black and we are proud of it. Growing up in Louisiana was hard because we had another layer between our Black, White, and Native relatives. There were those known as mulattoes, some of whom deny their Blackness to this day and deny any connection to us. While we knew our grandmothers, we never knew our grandfathers. I am Black because my dad was. My mother is Black only because she says she is! I believe Greg knew more about his family than I ever knew about mine and I'm still searching for the truth.

CHAPTER 2

SHE NEVER KNEW

Can you imagine being in high school, having great success in the sport you have chosen—and not just because you started out wanting to run track—but you did it because you wanted to insure having a shower every day?! Add to that, with all of your success, people all over town are talking about this kid they call Dick Gregory. He regretted not being able to explain to his mother what he really did in track and how important what he achieved was to his school at Sumner or at Southern Illinois University (SIU). His mother, Lucille, heard about the kid getting all the accolades around town and wished that could be her son! The only problem is that he chose not to tell his mom that Dick Gregory was her very own son, Richard! Why? He said she would not have believed him and since she didn't go to the school for anything regarding him or his activities she would not have understood. On the other hand, my mother knew about everything I did in school. If I didn't tell her, the principal or one of my teachers surely would have told her whether I wanted them to or not! Fortunately, I never had any bad reports! For real!

Greg's mother died young and never knew that the Dick Gregory people were talking about was her very own son. He knew at
his young age what he was up against in a racist system like the
one he always talked about in St. Louis. First, he said the school
record books did not list his name no matter what he did. In that
day, track was a sport reserved for white boys. Years later, he
would tell me, when describing the city in which he was born, that
whenever daylight savings time moved the time up, clocks moved
back in St. Louis! That, of course, was a joke. Still, he loved his
city and returned frequently for various causes. He also still has
family there, another reason he went back often.

Greg told me that one of the blessings of his life was going
to work with his mother sometimes, being able to sneak into the
room of the white people for whom his mother worked, and being
able to read some of the great books the family had. He learned
things from those books that he could never have imagined. He
never lost that love of books. He carried many of them around in
a backpack that often was so heavy with books and papers that it
strained his back, but he carried them anyway. Books and papers
were like a security blanket for him. He remembered so much of
what he read, but he still needed his books with him to show others
when he wanted to make a point. When he didn't have the right
book with him, he knew he could call me because whatever book
or paper he had, I, too, had a copy.

Years after his mother wished that track star would have been
her son, her son Richard became a super star in so many ways.
The world still called him Dick Gregory, but came to learn that
high school track star *was* Ms. Lucille's son, Richard, at Sumner
High School. He broke records there. He won the state cross
country championship in 1950, but that couldn't be proven by

the record books for no reason other than he was Black! At any rate, he won a track scholarship to Southern Illinois University and he set many records in track there. His mother died when he was twenty-one and he left college. My mom just made her transition when she was nearly ninety-nine years old. I dreaded thinking of living all these years without my mother, but at a very young age, he found himself without a mother and father in his life. After leaving SIU, Greg was drafted into the Army. As much as he hated war, being drafted was the only reason he went. Yet, it was in the Army that Greg earned a chance to do more comedy than he had previously done as a young man when he used comedy as a defense against young boys laughing at him! Once his Army tour was up, he briefly returned to SIU, but didn't stay. It became clear to him that the school was more interested in his running than in his studies. Upon leaving SIU, he decided to give professional comedy a try.

Greg went on to become a health guru, a civil rights activist, a human rights activist, a political activist, and a much sought-after counselor on many subjects. He also became a world-class humorist/comedian who influenced many comedians who came after him. And he became my best friend. Although many people thought of our being very different aside from our activism, he remained my best friend until the day he left this earth. Before and after meeting him, I've had many friends, but never one like him. He told me a lot of things he never told Ms. Lucille.

One example was never telling her a story about when he was a young boy trying to be a man. He and one of his young friends saw this gorgeous person and they both instantly fell in love. The person asked them if they would like to go to the drive-in theater sometime and they were both overjoyed to be asked and they glee-

fully said yes. I may be the only one who knew about that secret.
He said he never told others and no way was he going to tell his
mom. This one was long before his track fame, about which Ms.
Lucille never knew. As the time got closer for them to go to the
drive-in, he decided to go alone and tell his friend the "date" had
been cancelled. He then sneaked off so he could be alone with this
person. He was picked up at the appointed time. They arrived at
the drive-in and after a while, an arm went around him and he
was just lying back enjoying the moment when the person whispered to him in a very deep voice, *"What if I told you I'm a man?"*
Startled, he jumped up so fast to open the car door and get out of
the car, while seriously injuring his arm. He ran all the way home
with his arm in pain. He had a tough time explaining to his mom
how he'd injured his arm, but he made up something and never
told her or anybody what really happened that night! Again, Ms.
Lucille never knew!

CHAPTER 3

DIET FOR LIFE

As mentioned earlier, one night Greg called and asked if I would pick him up, and it wasn't from just down the street! He was asking me to pick him up from Baltimore on a Friday evening, the biggest traffic day of the week from Washington, D.C. to Baltimore! A lot of people can tell you about missing flights trying to go that route to Baltimore's Thurgood Marshall Airport. Ultimately, I did make it to his hotel and we made it back to my place. I have never regretted picking him up and driving him back to Washington. I have never regretted entertaining his friends for him so he could teach all of us how to make meatless burgers!

Greg convinced a lot of people to switch to a protein mix to make their burgers. Most of the burgers were made from black beans, so I guess you could call them "black bean burgers" on which he put loads of cheese! I never learned how much that diluted the health impact of the burger, but black bean became my favorite burger and my favorite bean soup! I still keep loads of black beans in my kitchen. The cheese was one of the only dairy products he used on anything. Now, when it came to mayonnaise and olive oil, I don't think he cared what was in them while he loaded nearly everything he ate with those condiments!

I am from Louisiana, so one would think I could cook soul food, but I can't; or maybe it's more appropriate to say, I don't cook it after learning how much of it damages our health. However, whatever I did cook, Greg considered it a treat. He always made me feel like I could cook anything well. He loved turnip bottoms, okra, onions with lots of seasoning over rice, eggplant, mashed potatoes, and deviled eggs! Lots of butter, olive oil, and mayonnaise were some of his sins. There was no limit to the amount he used. He rarely ate anything not on that list. For some reason he didn't like greens. That was a disappointment because I love greens and I have them at almost every meal, even with breakfast!

He was absolutely against our eating any kind of soy product. He believed soy caused many of the problems women had with our reproductive system and whether that was scientifically proven or not, I took no chances! I sure hated giving up my soy milk, soy ice cream, tofu burgers, etc., but if he said it wasn't good, I learned not to eat it, even if I didn't know why! Except for beef, before meeting him, there was little I wouldn't eat! I grew up on a typical southern soul food diet. Fortunately, we had all fresh food and no canned food. I still can't stand the taste of food coming out of a can. My mom preserved food, but it was always in glass jars!

Greg always advised against our drinking anything while eating. He said that took away the strength of our digestive juices. There was never a problem with that for me to this day. That was the practice while eating, but having a bit of bourbon and Coke before meals was okay! My drink of choice before meals however, was champagne! Without asking, he always ordered that for me, knowing it wouldn't go to waste. In all of those heavy bags on his shoulder, you can be sure there were bottles of water in some of them and he always advised people he met to drink more water, at least half of one's body weight. He said that water was necessary for many reasons. As the day goes by, he said that we lose water in many ways and need to replenish it often.

We need water to replenish what we lose through sweating, urinating, eliminating stool, even breathing. He said if we don't replace the water we lose, we become dehydrated and suffer from skin disorders by not drinking enough water. While he advised that we drink at least half of our body's weight, he acknowledged there are differences of opinion as to how much we need. He took no chances because he drank lots of water all day. While some people actually drink eight or more twelve-ounce bottles of water, he acknowledged there were ways to get some water through the food we eat, as well as through drinking it. Rather than quickly drinking down a lot of water at one time, he advised taking sips throughout the day. Obviously, he said, how much you drink depends upon where you live. A hot climate might require more water and whether you eat foods high in water might have an impact. If you exercise or sweat a lot are also determinants of how much you need to drink.

It took him hours to eat. He never just sat down to eat a meal. Mealtime was a ritual. In between bites, he called people, cussed them out, advised some on what they should do if they had a problem with their health, took some of his many vitamins, read something, fell asleep at the table, woke up and took a few more bites—you name it—but when he finished, he would help me with the dishes. I know that would be a bit hard to believe by most people, including his family! He was very thoughtful when it came to what to eat. He could eat the same thing every day if the meal included something he liked. I am the same way. Once I cook an item, I don't change meals until all of what I have already cooked is gone. That way I save on my utility bills!

Washing dishes was a ritual he seemed to relish. He told me he learned the proper way to wash dishes in the Army. He taught me that you first rinse the dishes, then you fix a dish pan of hot water with Clorox, allow the dishes to soak for a while, then put them in the dishwasher! By that time, it's time for the next meal! I did it while he was there, but when he wasn't, the dishes got lightly rinsed and placed in the dishwasher! I am like that little girl in the commercial who asks if you have to do all that, what is the dishwasher for?

He taught me that it is more important to be lovable than it is to be loved. I still have a hard time with that one, but he said, *"There are days when you just have to bow your head, say a prayer and let things go."* No matter how hard, I do that a lot and it takes away a lot of stress. Everything with which you disagree is just not worth stressing out over it.

Since Greg has been gone, his friend John Bellamy is developing a product for weight loss that was inspired by Greg because so many of our people struggle with their health, especially with their weight. The new product is called *The Caribbean Shake for Optimal Health*. The original product had been called *Bahamian Diet*.

People still call me to ask what vitamins I take, with the assumption I still take vitamins recommended by Greg. I do, but I usually refer them to practicing health care doctors that I know Greg approved. There is Doctah B, Glenn Ellis, Dr. Sakiliba Mines, Dr. James Dail and others. I have studied natural health, but I don't have a degree in it. I just read a lot and learned a lot from Greg. I still walk a lot—often as many as five miles per day—

just as he and I would walk. When people ask me what kind of medicine I take, I tell them I am a Dick Gregory disciple and I don't take medicine. I do, however, take vitamins. I rarely get sick and almost never have aches or pains!

My challenge still is drinking enough water. Greg carried his water around with him no matter where he went and I admit I haven't learned to do that often enough, but many of the people who came into contact with him still tell me how he helped them to improve their drinking of water. I get caught up in work and forget until it's too late in the evening. I also stay at the computer too long until I remember what he told me about taking breaks at least once per hour. I do remember to stretch a lot and I try to stay positive. I also try to stay away from negative thinking. Again, that is challenging some days, but I do try to practice the things he taught me.

With Greg's great interest in health, naturally, we attended the Congress the night the Affordable Care Act passed in March of 2010. When we arrived at the Capitol, the crowd was overwhelming. Fortunately, then Congressman Keith Ellison (now Minnesota's Attorney General) came through where we were trying to move to the balcony and recognized both of us. He grabbed our hand and told us to follow him. We squeezed through the crowd and Congressman Ellison got us all the way to seats in the balcony where visitors sat. We had a great view and watched the historic passage of what came to be known as "Obamacare." Leading up to the vote, I could send emails to friends in the White House, and I sent a note saying we should just call it "Obama Cares," so when they removed the "s" and just called it "Obamacare," I was ecstatic. It's likely whoever called it "Obamacare" first didn't even see my suggestion. I would like to think they did, but I was still happy with "Obamacare"—although I liked it better with the "s" on it! We just wanted the ACA to pass. We are still waiting for that better plan the Republicans promised. Most of them have tried only to destroy what President Obama did so that people who need it most would have no health plan.

CHAPTER 4

JUSTICE FOR ALL

Greg received many awards for his work. Very often, they wound up at my place. He had so many books, papers, and plaques at his place already that there was no room for any more. I have artwork, trophies, and other memorabilia people gave him. I even have his Hollywood Star poster. I tried to get it signed by the stars who were in attendance before he left us, but I still have several signatures to go. Among those who've signed are Jesse Buggs, Tommy Davidson, and me.

He did so much for civil rights, human rights, political rights, voting rights, and he never tired of speaking, marching, donating, and participating in all kinds of events to call attention to issues that would make life better for the least of God's children. He actively participated in so many movements for justice, and he had no fear about doing so. He often told me that whatever you fear controls you. That was fine with me, because being a Sagittarius, the word control could well be deleted from use. Any attempt to control me is like an invitation to not do what the controller is trying to do! Seeing his bravery so often just sealed my belief that fear should never stop anybody from doing the right thing. As a

result of that belief, I have walked up to a gunman and twisted
the gun from his hands and talked a gunman into standing down
with his gun or at least not to use it. I can't say I was totally without fear in either case, but the fear didn't control my intervention!

When Dr. Frances Cress-Welsing was having challenges just
to live comfortably in her home, and the District of Columbia
government did nothing to help her or to enforce its own laws,
Greg and I went to her home to inspect the disrespect being shown
to her by school officials next to her home and upheld by city officials. She could not live a comfortable life in her home during her
final years because of all the noise from the playground.

The noise from the school often chased her from her home
and kept her from getting rest. Noise was all around her all day.
Balls were continuously bouncing against her kitchen window and
into her yard. There was the noise all day from the playground
of the school that moved its operation right up against her home.
We took the matter to the District of Columbia government. They
were of no help and showed no sympathy. There was one Black
male on the committee. He was a total disappointment. He just
bowed his head, refused to look at us, and voted with those on
the committee against our appeal for help for Dr. Cress-Welsing.
There is no way he didn't know Dr. Cress-Welsing well enough
to come over and at least hear her side and explain why he could
not speak out for relief on her behalf, but he didn't.

The Zoning Commission didn't even uphold their own ruling
on her rightful expectation to enjoy the use of her property. The
Commission had earlier ordered the school to leave trees between
her home and the school playground and to put up a sound barrier
to keep down some of the noise. That never happened and as a
matter of fact, the trees were cut down! No sound barrier was

ever built. To add insult to injury, after purchasing the property on one side of her home, the school bought the property on the other side of her home, thus causing more noise. Her home was practically surrounded by the school and the noise. Only one City Councilman acknowledged receiving our request for assistance to Dr. Cress-Welsing. That was Phil Mendelson, but even he did not help us to get relief for her. She died before we could help her or assist her in regaining the enjoyment of her home. I believe the stress of that situation hastened her death because she could rarely get away from the noise unless she left her home to go elsewhere.

CHAPTER 5

AFRICAN/AFRICAN-AMERICAN ACTIVISM

Greg was the consummate activist. No one became involved in as many issues as he did. He didn't mind going to jail to bring attention to the cause in which he was involved. His activism didn't just take place in the United States. He went to Iran to work on the hostage release when Jimmy Carter was President. We went to London to work on the BP (British Petroleum) case and, naturally, we went out to the predominantly Black section of London to listen to their challenges. Well, as we left London, revolts over inequality there began, and a lot of the city burned. Trust me, we had nothing to do with that!

While we took several trips abroad, the most memorable one was to Senegal in Africa where we participated in Rev. Leon Sullivan's African/African American Summit. We took a train to New Jersey to get our flight to Senegal. We had an airplane full of friends from all around the country, including the late Rev. Joseph Lowery, Rev. Jesse Jackson, and other Black leaders. Late that night on the flight when almost everyone was asleep, there was a rumbling where everyone suddenly woke up. Someone had gone to the area where movies could be shown on the flight, and they'd set up one that was obviously not meant to be shown to a lot of regular church leaders and attendees! There were a lot of them on the flight.

No one ever owned up to the X-rated movie, but that is the situation that got our trip to Senegal started and everybody was wide awake after the movie and joking about the contents of it. We arrived in Senegal the following morning and were taken directly to our hotels. We were eager to get checked in and to go back to the airport to greet Commerce Secretary Ron Brown. We were all so proud of him, greeting him at the airport was like greeting a rock star. We traveled to Senegal with a lot of other people who were also going to the African/African American Summit that was held in different African nations annually. Ron did not fly with us. He flew to Senegal on a government airplane and all of us who were Americans came to the airport to welcome him. We were devastated when he later died in that airplane crash. Greg always believed the crash was planned. He later went to jail for protesting the handling of the crash. He believed the airplane had been shot down.

While we were in Senegal, Greg went over to Goree Island with a group of friends. As soon as he came back to the hotel, he was so moved by the experience that he immediately called me and told me I had to go there, too. He went back with me that same night. We had to travel by boat. As soon as we arrived, I teared up just thinking about how our ancestors got there and what happened to them upon their arrival on the island.

Greg had friends in Senegal, so after greeting Secretary Brown, we went into the city to visit with his friends. We went to a tailor and ordered clothing to be made while we were in the country. They were later delivered to our hotel. Unfortunately, my outfit had problems, but I didn't have time to go back to the shop for adjustments, so I never wore the suit. I did, however, have a beautiful yellow African-inspired outfit to take home that a Nigerian brother had brought along from Nigeria and gave to me. I wound up gifting it to my good friend Georgia Maryland (nicknamed "2 States") when I returned home. She absolutely loved African-inspired clothing and I knew she would wear it more than I.

Before and after the trip to Senegal, I had an opportunity to visit Gabon, Benin, South Africa and Cote Ivoire. Greg and I later had an invitation to visit with the President of Equatorial Guinea. For once, I didn't read in advance anything about the President or his country. We dined at the home of Hope Sullivan whose father was Dr. Leon Sullivan who started the African/African American Summits.

After the elaborate dinner, I was asked to serve as the leader to coordinate the programs exclusively for women from around the world who would attend the next Summit to be held in Equatorial Guinea. I accepted the invitation knowing nothing about the country. Well, upon telling Greg about the invitation, he in no uncertain terms vetoed the trip. I was so disappointed, but whenever he said no, I knew he had good reasons. He sent me to do research on the President and his son. That was an awakening, and I knew I couldn't be a part of the event, especially not as a special guest of the government. I declined the invitation but was grateful I had been considered. I am sure it was Hope who selected and recommended me and I was grateful for her recommendation, but my conscience and Greg's objection would not allow me to do it.

CHAPTER 6

SOMEONE WE COULD LOOK UP TO

Even though he's made his transition, Greg's life is still one to whom people look for answers. I know I did and still do many times. I never heard him say, "I don't know." I don't think that was in his vocabulary. He spoke to so many people and when anybody asked for help, he gladly gave advice. He wrote so many books. He did so many recorded shows. People heard from him so many times that his advice is still sought on many subjects. I get asked often what he would have said about various things. There is a general assumption that he told me about a lot of things—and he did—but I didn't necessarily remember all of them and I would never try to make up things he said.

I try to use my radio program and other media appearances, my regular weekly writings, and my speaking engagements to remind people what he said on so many subjects and what he did that still benefits us all. When I listen to people who knew him, I collect things he told them, and on all of my radio programs, I ask my guests if they knew him and/or if they remember anything he said or did. They almost always do and relish telling their Dick Gregory stories.

Even when people had never met Greg in person, they've heard about him, or they remember something he said or did. I've seen men run up to him on the way to his car after a program he's on and eagerly tell something about being present when he spoke at their college or university years ago. These are people of all races and cultures, mostly men, but women have their stories, too!

I had Ms. Linda Dakin-Grimm, author of *Dignity and Justice: Welcoming the Stranger at our Border,* on my radio program called "Wake Up and Stay Woke!" and I kind of assumed she might not know a lot about him. I always ask my guests if they had heard of anything he might have said. She immediately spoke up to indicate she had never met him in person, but she knew that he always spoke truth to power in an era where that was impossible to do (safely), but he did it anyway. She indicated knowing how much he supported women and women's issues. I was pleased to hear her saying so much of what I knew about him.

On the same day that I had Ms. Dakin-Grimm on my program, I asked John Fairman, CEO of Delta Health Center, Inc. in Mississippi the same question. He was one of many personal friends to Greg, so I knew he would be speaking from experience. He indicated that Greg had taught him to practice drinking water to equal his body's weight. He also said Greg had taught him to have faith in the Universal God. He said Greg was a blessing to his life.

I remember Greg talking about having a good friend in Dallas, Texas who always invited him to do a program for her. I didn't meet her until after he left us. I've had her on my show and I have come to know her well. Learning about her work, it's obvious that she, too, is a Dick Gregory disciple. Her work in her community certainly indicates that. She promotes a lot of community service through her newspaper. Here is what she said when I asked her if she knew him or remembered anything he said or did, *"It couldn't have been anybody else but me that he was talking about!"* That was Cheryl Smith, publisher of a Metro Dallas newspaper. When he left us, I saw her newspaper and she honored him by creating a cover on her newspaper that looked like a monument to him! She continues to use lots of his photos on the cover, and I know that anyone who knew Greg and saw her paper would pick it up to see what the paper was all about even if they'd never seen it previously!

Julieanna Richardson, Founder and CEO of The History Makers was one of my guests and when I asked her my usual question, she responded first with having tried to get him to sit for an interview for her collection, but got nowhere with him. My neighbor, Amy Billingsley, asked for my help to get him to do that. He didn't hesitate. He showed up at my place on the appointed day, sat from 6:00 p.m. to 1:00 a.m. and did what she said was one of The HistoryMakers' most fascinating interviews. She said he told her one of the stories about his growing up and someone brought a turkey by for one of the holidays. As much as his family needed food, he was so insulted and humiliated by that so he told the person bringing the turkey they could just take it right on back because they had no stove on which to cook the turkey. He was not being rude or ungrateful. He was being truthful.

CHAPTER 7

OTHER ACTIVISM

Greg was an activist from his early days in school in St. Louis. He enjoyed talking about his activism at Sumner High School. Track was his key sport and into late life, he rarely missed a track meet on television or any place he could find one.

He was a popular student and athlete. He even led protests and walkouts about the school never using Black graduation paraphernalia makers for things like class photos, class yearbooks, and class rings. Class rings were very meaningful during that time. That was the only graduation many students would have, and the ring was a witness to that accomplishment. Track was his key sport. I could still hear the sadness in his voice when he told me about his days as an athlete at Sumner and why he began running track. He said that was his way of getting a regular shower as a member of the team, though there was no equality no matter how good he was as a member of the team. He was the first African American to win the Missouri State cross country championship. He was hurt when his name did not appear in the record book for his feats for no other reason than his being Black.

It seems he had to fight for everything, and he didn't wait until he was an adult to begin his concern about injustices. That was a lifelong concern and he risked everything for it. He fought not just for himself, but also for others. He had to think and he had to organize to be successful. I get tears just thinking about some of the challenges he faced much of his life.

Greg said when you just protest, burn and tear things down, you are not revolting—you are rioting. He held this view for the rest of his life. He preferred the act of revolting and for that you had to organize. At Sumner, whatever anyone thought of him, he organized for better and less crowded conditions in his school. He was always conscious of right and wrong and was willing to go to bat for the underdog.

From his track notoriety at Sumner, he earned a track scholarship and went to Southern Illinois University at Carbondale. There, he set many records, as he had at Sumner. He ran the mile and the half mile. Everything wasn't rosy at Carbondale. He still experienced racism. With all of the running he did, his mother still didn't know that hero at Sumner was her son. She died not knowing he was the one setting all the records because white people decided to change his name from the name she gave him—Richard Claxton Gregory—to Dick Gregory. I guess that sounded whiter than Richard because his Blackness had no value to them! He said if he'd told his mother he was the Dick Gregory everybody was talking about, she would have thought he was lying. So, he never told her.

Greg was prominent in the Civil Rights Movement. He was prominent in the Kent State University protests. He was prominent in protests against police violence against Black people. He was prominent in the protests against the Vietnam War. He was prominent in Indian fishing rights and all kinds of injustices. Lil, his wife, with whom he had eleven children, had been involved in many of these causes, too. At one point, he was criticized for basically being an absent father, but he had an answer for that. He said, relating to his critics, that Hitler and many criminals had fathers at home and did nothing good for humanity. After all, he wasn't away from home for trivial reasons. He was away making things better for all of humanity.

I once read an article by a woman by the name of Marilyn Thomas who had a picture with him in her office at Alabama A&M University. When one of her students asked if the picture in her office was her father, she said, "For a few seconds, I felt proud that this mistake of identity was made. You may be wondering why I wasn't more shocked or why I didn't proceed to take out a photograph of my own father. I had no father to speak of really; he had never been in my life." Like Ms. Thomas, so many people relied on Greg to at least be an acting father and consulted him on so many things.

After I came to know him, we went to so many rallies and supported so many causes together and separately in the United States and abroad that I won't try to count them. Since I was a little girl, my mother had taught me how to be a community activist and to work against what I saw as wrong. He taught me to be fearless in doing so.

Greg returned to St. Louis often to help his city, his family, and his high school. One of those high school celebrations always took place the weekend of the major event of the National Congress of Black Women (NCBW). Even if he showed up late at the NCBW event, he always honored us by making it back to Washington before we concluded. Of course, walking into an event late was no stranger to him! Whenever he arrived anywhere, people were overjoyed to see him. Year after year, many organizations invited him back to their conferences and conventions.

Greg said he started joking while very young because people laughed at him about various things having to do with his being poor—about his having to wear whatever he had around the house to go outside to play. Sometimes, he even had to wear an old dress because he had nothing else, and that's when kids would really laugh at him and point at him. So, he would just hurl a joke back at them to take the attention off him. It was not until he was in the Army that he really began serious joking. His entertaining of the troops sort of became his job while he was in the Army and that was just fine with him. He served in the military with Speaker Nancy Pelosi's brother, and it seems that he kept her brother out of trouble! He never told me what the trouble was that he could or did get into, but just thinking of him keeping somebody out of trouble sounds funny when I think of how mischievous he was! All I know is that Nancy seemed to have great appreciation for whatever he did, and she always seemed glad to see him.

After Greg became a comedy star, he later got involved in the Civil Rights Movement and that's where he became a true soldier, a real warrior for civil and human rights. He always credited Lil with her role in the Movement. I will never forget the night I first learned of his courage and who he really was. I was a teacher in South Central Los Angeles, very near where what was called the Watts Riot, Revolt, or Uprising (called by all the names by different people) was going on. That occurred between August 11–15 in 1965. I remember being at a Delta Sigma Theta Convention in Los Angeles at the time at the Ambassador Hotel where I first met and found myself sitting beside no less than Lena Horne, one of my Delta Sigma Theta sisters. She gave me a beautiful auto-graphed photograph. I was unable to get home because I lived in the area of the dangerous activity. Greg was in Los Angeles at the time and he knew about the conflict, and actually walked into a crowd where shots were being fired.

He was shot in the leg on the way to his efforts to calm things down and in spite of his injury, he just kept on walking toward what was going on! I didn't meet him in person that far back, but that was my introduction to who he was and how courageous he was. I was a teacher at Carver Jr. High, a school not far away from the action, and after seeing what he did, I got up the courage to walk around the school campus with my principal to keep him out of danger. I knew a lot of the young men in the area and just didn't believe they would hurt me! Though he was not involved in the activity that night, one of my students from that time was Mark Ridley-Thomas. I'm told he may have changed, for better or worse—depending on what the issue is—but he was one of my sweetest little 7th graders in my class at Carver Jr. High School.

It was believed Greg had been shot by someone in the crowd, not by the police. Instead of falling and calling for help, he just said something like, "All right, goddamnit. You shot me. Now go home." That was the big news that night. Dick Gregory had been shot trying to calm a situation. He never ran away from a dangerous situation. There was always hope that he could help. I, too, tend to run toward dangerous situations when others run away, thinking there might be something I could do to help. That's something we had in common. It could be said that that is what attracted me to him and him to me. We were always game for trying things when many others said, "No way." We often talked about some of our leaders who showed up for the cameras in their suits and fancy words and then went home. When we were in a situation, we were there for the long haul even when we heard about the danger of what we were doing.

Dr. Martin Luther King, Jr. came to Los Angeles about the end of the Watts revolt in 1965, which Greg told me was a riot, not a revolt. He told me a revolt means you have plans for what is to be done afterwards, but a riot is just tearing down things. I think Dr. King would have agreed with the damage done in Los Angeles after he viewed it. At any rate, Dr. King was known for supporting nonviolence. He was convinced the Southern Christian Leadership Conference should begin to do work in northern urban areas, but saw a difference in why the protests and the South were different. He met with various community leaders. He said the protests in the South were about dignity and rights, while the ones in urban cities were about things like inadequate housing, inadequate jobs, economic opportunities, and equality of opportunities. His discussion with us led to his going back to Washington, D.C. to talk with President Lyndon Johnson and the War on Poverty was launched from that meeting. While I was aware of Greg's activism, I didn't meet him in person until many years later.

When I ran for Congress in 1986, I was often knowingly going into dangerous situations. Like what Greg often did by not running for himself, but for the causes of others, I wasn't running for Congress in the dangerous terrain of Louisiana for myself. I was running for our people at the urging of my then best friend for years, Congressman Mervyn Dymally. I was just out of law school and looking forward to starting a law practice. I was determined to be a civil and human rights lawyer! In fact, I had never thought of running for any office anywhere, even though I had been asked by others to run for various offices. After struggling through law school, the first thing I wanted to do the most was to go out and make a lot of money! I had to give that dream up in order to run for office, however. Black people still thank me for the effort and often when I return to their communities, they treat me like royalty.

Prior to my running, Louisiana had no Black members of Congress. No one was even running, but when I ran, apparently, they saw that a Black person could win. Since I ran for Congress, Louisiana has had three Black members of Congress. Cleo Fields of Baton Rouge decided to run after I ran, and I shared my materials and experience with him. Then came Bill Jefferson of New Orleans, and more recently, Cedric Richardson of New Orleans. Cedric is now Senior Adviser to President Biden. For the past few years, Louisiana has elected more than twenty Black female Mayors and many to the State Legislature. In the 2020 election season, Adrian Perkins ran a great race for the U.S. Senate and Sandra "Candy" Christophe has run for the U.S. Congress in much of the area in which I ran, though many of the towns have been deleted and others added. I am pleased to see how many Black people now run for other than local races since I ran. I donate to their campaigns and share with them my experience and advice when they ask.

I certainly don't take credit for influencing all of those who ran since I ran, but many tell me I inspired them. They, too, inspire me in many ways because I know what it's like running for office in many areas of Louisiana where even some mulattoes don't consider Black people worthy of a handshake! Yeah, we still have that three colors problem there! I've had hands jerked away when I reached out and I've been referred to as the "cullud" woman and the "Nigger Woman" and probably some more names that didn't come to my attention. But, despite all of it, I soldiered on and a lot of good things came out of the race.

I have done my part for the cause by running for Congress years ago when few Black people were doing so anywhere. Though I have been asked many times, I have no plans to run for public office ever again, but I can look back on my running over thirty years ago and be glad I did. That race is what allowed me to meet in person the one and only Dick Gregory. I get calls from people who are thinking of running for something all around the country and they call me to get advice. I always stop and talk with them. When I am at my mother's home in Louisiana, they stop by to chat about my experience, and frequently ask for my advice. When some know I am visiting my mom, they pass by and just blow their car horn to let me know they still appreciate the ground I broke in Louisiana politics. Greg always showed his appreciation for people who helped him along the way. I pray that I will always do the same.

Greg rose from poverty in St. Louis and became an awesome comedian, health expert, and civil and human rights activist. He was highly successful in all three areas and though he's gone, people still search for advice or for responses he has given in the past. Since he's been gone, a woman who knew both of us called and even asked me what he would have advised her to do to have a baby without the usual way of having a man in her life! People knew that as much as we were together, he had shared a lot of things with me, but that was not one of them!

Greg had several shows where he was still called on to teach on various subjects and he worked up to the very week he passed away. He was still in demand. When he heard people say, *"America, love it or leave it,"* he simply replied, *"I won't love it because it's not a*

friendly country, and I won't leave it until I personally straighten it out."
The night he left us, I sat by his bedside and promised him I would
do all I could to work on his goals and our joint goals. I may not
be able to finish that race for him, but he left me with the motiva-
tion to do all that I can to join others in moving the needle toward
justice in many areas. Occasionally, I think the effort is a losing
battle, but I keep on trying. I try to remember how he encouraged
me to never lose the faith and to keep my eyes on the prize.

While he didn't live to complete that promise of equal rights
for all, he left a whole lot of us here who are still running to situations in which we know he would have been involved and working
on his promise. He would be pleased to witness the progress the
Black Lives Matter movement and others are making. When he
passed away, I am told that people went to his Hollywood star to
visit and placed flowers on it in memory of him. His star is located
at 1650 Vine Street in Hollywood. He was honored in a ceremony
on February 2nd, 2015.

Recently, I was asked by Marlena Tracey of Covenant House
to participate in the *Sleep Out Movement* to raise funds for homeless
youth. I immediately agreed. As soon as the event was announced,
Dr. Theresa Buckson sent me a note saying, *"No way should you be
sleeping out in this cold."* Dr. Christian Gregory called with the same
basic message. I was having a hard time dealing with backing out
of such an event, even though anytime the weather goes under
70, I'm cold and the weather was a long way under 70 that night!
Christian informed me that the weather would be 39 degrees on
the night of the event but in the spirit of Dick Gregory, I was going
to do this because I know this is the kind of event he would have
no hesitation to join. As I was agonizing over the decision, based
upon what Greg would have done, a message came from Cove-

nant House informing me there was a change of plans due to city regulations and CDC guidelines and only a limited number of people would be allowed to participate. I was being asked to speak at the pre-Sleep Out and there would be a virtual opportunity for the actual Sleep Out! At times like that, I truly believe Greg was taking charge to say, *You don't have to do this to keep a promise to me.* The only other explanation for the change of plans would be Dr. Buckson and Dr. Gregory knew I shouldn't be spending the night out in freezing weather, no matter what my promise was!

CHAPTER 8

THE BRITISH PETROLEUM (BP) OIL SPILL

In the middle of President Barack Obama's first term as President, there was an explosion off the coast of Louisiana, creating perhaps what was the most disastrous oil spill in the history of the industry. For seven years before Greg left us, Art Rocker, Greg, and I worked on getting justice for those injured physically or in their businesses and churches. Many never received what they deserved, but not because we didn't spend years trying to help them. Since Greg left us, Art and I continued the fight for victims up to 10 years after the tragedy. Through it all, Kenneth Feinberg who was called the "Pay Czar," initially hired for millions of dollars to oversee the case, continued to promise poor and marginalized people would be compensated. Many died from toxins spewed as a result of the oil spill, but neither they nor their families received anything. Art, Greg, and I traveled all over the states where poor people were impacted by the tragedy to no avail for at least ten years.

We enlisted the help of Congresswoman Sheila Jackson Lee who tried to help, again, to no avail. We contacted Congressman Emanuel Cleaver who at the time was leader of the Congressional Black Caucus. Art and Greg traveled to Kansas City to meet with him, but nothing happened. We attended hearings in Washington but got no help. We picketed. We negotiated ad nauseam. We sought the help of various Black leaders who gave no help, but we saw evidence of their accepting money for their various causes from British Petroleum, the company that had put 20 billion dollars in an escrow fund under pressure from the White House; yet, nothing happened for poor and marginalized people. At the time, NAACP President Dr. Cornell Brooks was the only person who responded to our request for active and public Black leadership support.

Art Rocker, Head of People for Peace, Chief of Police (now Mayor) Jimmy Gardner of Pritchard, Alabama, Greg, and I went to London, England to the British Petroleum Headquarters, seeking satisfaction for the losses of people's property during that devastating oil spill. So many lost their jobs and even lives during the BP Oil Spill. We kept getting bounced around in the United States, from New Orleans to Houston and finally to London, spending thousands of dollars and our time trying to help the victims.

When all of the British Petroleum officials seemed to be out of town upon our arrival in London, we decided to picket them. We were not allowed in the building, so we made our signs and drew attention to our cause outside. I don't know how they found that one Black person to come to the door of the British Petroleum headquarters to tell us we would not be allowed in the building and we should return home to get a response from their officials back in the United States. After picketing the company for a while, we took a tour of London, visited a heavily Black section, then returned to the U.S. We kept going back to Houston, to Ken Feinberg's office in Washington, D.C., and any other place we could talk with a British Petroleum official. By the way, it's easy to notice that BP stations are all over the Black community where the people we were trying to help lived. We picketed BP in Houston. Although we stayed on their case, Black and marginalized people never got paid fairly. Ultimately, we did get some help for some of the impacted communities. Not nearly what they deserved, but some got something. Most got nothing. I still never stop at a BP station. I don't think we should spend our money with companies that have no respect for Black people.

I will never forget that two-week trip Greg and I took, along with Art Rocker on a part of it, during the British Petroleum oil spill aftermath. We'd formed a group to try to help people who'd been injured by the oil spill, but had no idea how to collect for the damages. There were many trips in between, but on this particular trip, Greg and I flew to New Orleans to meet Art Rocker. We participated in meetings regarding the impact of the oil spill, then drove to Pritchard, Alabama where we met then Pritchard Police Chief Jimmy Gardner, who later became Mayor, and others. We listened to damages done there and drove on to Mobile where we heard from others who'd been harmed. I was always called on to speak, but everywhere we went, Dick Gregory, without a doubt, was the star of the show. Crowds came out to hang onto his every word.

From Mobile, we went on to Pensacola, where Art Rocker had us meet a lot of his friends and associates, among them a lot of Patels! There are a lot of Patels in Florida. For Indians, that name is sort of like Black people being named Johnson or Smith or Jones! We visited one of the Patel Hotels. We left Art in Pensacola because that is where he lived. Greg and I rented an SUV where we (or should I say I) drove on to Gainesville, Florida where we were to speak at Florida A&M University that evening. I had never previously driven such a big automobile so that was a challenge. The SUV was totally packed with all of Greg's luggage. Before we arrived at the University, a member of AFSCME met us and without our knowledge had planned a rally regarding the oil spill, and we were immediately hijacked and pulled into it. Naturally, Greg's adoring crowd gathered around every place we went. I was tired, but I endured the extra stop. That night, we spoke at the University, returned to the hotel, and I wasted no time going to bed. After all, it had become obvious that instead of our sharing the driving for the two weeks to make the many stops along the way, I would be doing all of the driving! I was okay with that because I knew Greg would be doing most of the talking wherever we stopped!

The next morning, I quickly packed and took my luggage downstairs. I gave the valet Greg's room number and asked him to go up to get Greg's bags. So he took one of those small carts and started to go up. I advised him he would need a larger one. He waved me off and said the one he had would be okay. When he came back to the lobby bearing eleven bags for Greg, he said, "Wow, that's a record!" I had tried to warn him!

Greg slept most of the trip as I drove. We went from Gainesville to Lakeland in Polk County, Florida as the skies just opened up and the rain came pouring down like I have rarely seen. As I struggled to see the road while we drove into Lakeland, Greg woke up and asked, "Do you want me to drive?" We were already there, so my response begged to use the kind of language he so often employed, but I didn't. He never heard me use an offensive word, but I heard him use a lot! We had a wonderful meeting that evening with our Polk County Chapter that was chaired by

Doris Moore-Bailey. This was our largest chapter in the National Congress of Black Women at the time.

While in Polk County, we were directed to a spontaneous meeting on the Saturday morning that was arranged by Ted Terry who had added the event while we were already on the road with the owner of a vitamin shop who knew we would be in her area. Needless to say, it seems that everybody who heard Greg would be at that pharmacy showed up to pack the place. Naturally, this extra stop went overtime, considering we were to be in yet another town soon.

We went on to speak at Bethel AME Church in Lakeland on the Saturday afternoon from which I had to practically drag him away, knowing I had to drive on to St. Petersburg in Pinellas County, Florida where Greg was to speak that night. We got there and the place was so crowded that everybody could not get in. The owner asked if we would come back on the next morning, Sunday, to speak for those who could not get in. I am thinking, "Oh no, I have to drive to West Palm Beach for an event!" On the other hand, Greg didn't hesitate to agree to the added Sunday morning show. Same thing—very crowded. Stayed well overtime and, again, I was thinking about our long drive to West Palm Beach and on to Miami for events in both places that evening. It didn't seem to bother Greg as I drove and drove, often through rain!

We finally left far later than we should have. It seems that I drove forever that day over bridges that went straight up, then straight down and I hated that! I have never liked driving over bridges. I know he taught me that whatever you fear is what controls you if you allow it to do so. He also told me that fear and God do not occupy the same space, so I just held tightly onto the steering wheel, pretending I wasn't scared, assuming God was with me, and I kept on moving until the bridges were behind us!

When I was sufficiently tired as he slept in the car, I stopped by an alligator pit and admired how they moved around behind the fence. He missed my whole adventure. I had no fear of the alligators because I thought the fence protected me against them. After resting for a while, I went back to the car and we were on the road again. I was later told what horrified me, "Wow, you know those alligators have been known to jump over the fence where you stopped?" Too late, no fear! It might have been a different story if I had been told that while I was standing at the fence observing them!

From the alligator area, we went through a lot of rain. We drove into West Palm Beach right on time, held a meeting with some women who were interested in joining the National Congress of Black Women, then drove on to Miami where we were met by Tony Wilson, known as *Young James Brown*. That night, Tony took us to a club, and I still don't understand how so many people got in there. The performers had to step around people sitting on the floor just to find a place to perform. Tony did his James Brown act. I made a few remarks, but all those people were there to see Dick Gregory. For some reason, we could not get a flight out of Miami the next day, so we wound up having to drive back to Orlando to catch a plane.

I will never forget the time in Washington, D.C. when we were picketing near the Willard Hotel. I was scheduled to speak for the funeral of former City Councilwoman Nadine Winter. No matter what Greg did, the police would not arrest him, which is something he wanted to do to call attention to the cause of the people we represented from the tragic BP oil spill. I tried to explain to the police what we were doing, so they *would* arrest him! They continued to tell me, "You know we are not going to arrest Mr. Gregory." I begged them to arrest him, so I could get to the funeral. They didn't budge. I know you've probably never heard of a person's lawyer begging the police to have her client arrested, but I did. The funeral could not wait, and someone was already calling me to let me know they were near my place on the program.

Finally, Greg escalated his protest by blocking the door to the building. He tied his hands to the door, so they finally arrested him. At that point, I ran to the other side of the building where the police were taking him to the transport car and joined the group chanting, "Don't take him away! Pay the checks!" As soon as they loaded him into the police car, I had my nephew, Troy, drive my car around and rush me to the church where the funeral was held. I ran into the church and they immediately called me up to make my remarks in my tee shirt and tennis shoes. I had every intention to change into appropriate clothing for the funeral, but it turned out to be go-as-you-are or miss the funeral. Once I explained the situation, I assumed the people would understand.

When I looked out in the audience, I saw a whole line of seats filled with high-ranking police officers, politicians and family members of Ms. Winter. All I could think of to begin my remarks was, "Do you know how hard it is to get Dick Gregory arrested in this town?" The police, the Winter family and everybody in the church were laughing hard as I continued. As soon as I finished my tribute to Ms. Winter, I asked to be excused to rush over to the jail where Greg and our friend, Art Rocker, were taken when they were arrested. At the desk, I asked to see Mr. Gregory and a police officer from the back of the room, yelled, "He don't want to get out!" I knew that, but I was finally allowed to see him. There, I found the arresting officers back in the cellblock with Greg and Art laughing, talking and asking all kinds of questions about health-care and anything that came to their minds. When they finally decided they had to get back to work and left the cellblock, they left the cell door open, but locked the door behind them to the main office. Greg wanted to stay—again to get publicity for our cause—so he just laid down on that hard jail bench in the cell and went to sleep.

I needed to leave, but the door outside the cell leading to the lobby was locked and I was getting no answer from the front desk and they weren't answering the phone. I had to call my sister Bernice who was a few blocks away to come and tell them at the front desk that I wanted to leave because Greg was scheduled to receive an award that evening. He wanted me to go, accept it on his behalf, and make remarks for him. I rushed home, got dressed and on my way out of the house, I received a call from a police lieutenant where Greg was being held. He said, "Ma'am, you should come to pick up Mr. Gregory because a judge has ordered us to let him out of jail!" I am thinking, "Oh no, after all I have done to get him arrested!" I rushed over to the jail, picked him up, and we dashed off to the event where he was receiving the award. He'd be able to speak for himself. Upon the presentation of the award, he was allowed to make comments, meant to be two to three minutes in length! Well, those comments went on and on and on long past three or five or even ten minutes.

I moved around the room to several different spaces to get his attention and to signal him that he was there to make a few acceptance remarks and not to do a full show! When I moved to the back of the room, giving all kind of signals for him to stop, he said, "I see you, Baby" and continued his talk until he was ready to stop. That's the way it always was. I would give the signals and he would call me out and continue talking. The audience didn't seem to mind, but after I had been picketing all day, dashing off to a funeral, running over to the police station, rushing home to get dressed, figuring out what I was going to say on his behalf, going back to the jail to pick him up, and rushing to the event, I was in no mood for a long speech, even if the people in the audience were laughing at his every utterance.

Later on, we had to go to court to defend him against trespassing charges. The judge ordered a drug test among other things. Can you imagine a judge ordering Dick Gregory to take a drug test? But that's what happened! He had to sign a document before we left the courtroom regarding payment for any charges. He really did as he often joked about doing. He signed it with *Your Mama* instead of his name! In his performances, he often told the crowd he did that. Well, as one of his lawyers, I know he really did that, but no judge ever mentioned it. We went to the building where he was told to go to take the drug test. We thought that was hilarious, but he took the test anyway. It came back *uncertain!*

We knew he had no illegal drugs in his body, so we just waited for the testers to figure out what was going on. No one could determine what was in his system. We knew it was nothing more than all the vitamins he was using. There was no way there would be any illegal drugs in his system. We waited for the results. The drug testers never figured out what was there and we didn't give them any clues. The case was finally dismissed. As a matter of fact, I was sitting in the courtroom ready to defend the case when the marshal sent someone in to tell me that they had taken him out from a side door so he didn't have to come back into the courtroom.

Greg was free to leave! He walked out of the court to a lot of high fives and words of endearment from all of his loyal fans who were lined up against the wall as he passed by to walk out of the building. It was useless for me to prepare to defend him, but I always did just in case there was a trial. He had already said goodbye to all the young brothers back in the cellblock waiting for their time before the judge. They were all so excited to see him. He was treated royally back there. A marshal had even offered to get him some tea or some water, not knowing he would never have accepted it. He never took chances on whether someone was friend or foe, but I am sure these marshals were friends. He had experienced several times when someone had tried to harm him, so he never took chances on eating just anywhere. He told me of the time he was in a hotel and while he was out of the room, someone came in and left some women's clothing and shoes in his room. He promptly took them down to the front desk to show them what someone had tried to do. By taking that step, he was saved from an attempted embarrassment.

I wrote a letter to certain Black leadership, seeking support for Black people who were in deep pain as a result of the 2010 British Petroleum Oil Spill. I asked them to notice how long after the oil spill that Black people had never received relief. Businesses had closed. People had died. Churches had lost tithes as they tried to be of service to the people in their communities.

As you may recall, in a special program aired by Oprah Winfrey on January 18th, 2015, called *14 Civil Rights Legends Who Paved the Way for Us All*, she aired the video that showed Dick Gregory as one of those who gave his all to make BP live up to its promise to the poor. On his dying bed, I vowed to continue this effort we'd worked on from the beginning of the oil spill together until BP made good on keeping its promise to pay the poor and underserved for the damage the oil spill did to them. A few months after the oil spill, we were asked to organize the underserved and underrepresented, who'd been damaged by the BP Oil Spill. Greg, Art Rocker (President of Operation People for Peace), and I (President of the National Congress of Black Women, Inc. and The Dick Gregory Society) began efforts to get people and the Black churches on the Gulf Coast that were damaged by the disastrous BP oil spill paid for their suffering and losses.

After many meetings with BP officials on behalf of the people, we were promised everyone would be paid by BP; however, while large corporations and businesses had been paid, marginalized and underserved people and their churches (most of which are African Americans) had not been paid.

At the urging of Attorney Kenneth Feinberg, BP Czar, who initially was handling claims, we collected all information in accordance with a formula given to us by Mr. Feinberg from those who suffered losses and we were promised they would be paid. Despite promises from all BP executive leadership in London, Houston, Washington and New Orleans where we traveled, those promises to pay have not been kept these many years later. Billions of dollars have been allocated to pay for damages caused by the BP oil spill to big companies, yet promises have not been kept for poor people. We made effort after effort to no avail.

We asked many leaders if they would be kind enough to assist us in urging BP to keep their promise that they made to Dick Gregory who fasted, went to jail, and traveled hundreds of miles to resolve this matter. We thought a letter from them would make a powerful statement of support, along with other letters from leaders in our community, to fulfill BP's unkept promise to the poor and underserved. As one drives through Black communities, they can see BP stations everywhere and BP makes a huge amount of money from these stations. BP has paid billions of dollars in claims but has yet to keep their promise to the poor. We kept on calling for help as we had done earlier to no avail. We again asked for letters of support for our efforts.

We gave the address for the person who should receive the letter. We sent this letter of request to so many Black leaders requesting support for poor people who were suffering from diseases and various losses—even of life. How many letters of support do you think we received? Still, Dr. Cornell Brooks, who at the time was President of the NAACP, sent the only letter of support. I can't say we sent the letter to all Black leaders and it would be easy for any one of them to say they didn't receive the letter. That may be true, but they were aware of the problem and we never saw any of them on the protest lines with us or in the corporate suites as we bargained what we could. Sadly, too many chose to receive *donations* from BP! That is a big problem in our community. Greg and I could be rich if we ever took payoffs to forget the matter. We certainly had our share of payoff offers—even in the millions—but we said no. BP ultimately gave a few community grants but not worth nearly as much as the poor victims were owed.

We went to court a few more times, but the result was always the same: CASE DISMISSED!

CHAPTER 9

THE ENTERTAINER

Going to court for one thing or the other was never all that far away. I can't count all the times I have attended one of Greg's professional performances, so much so that he once told me I could very well do his show for him! I didn't get carried away with his confidence in me on that, but I did begin to use humor in my speeches. He had great respect and admiration for many other entertainers. One was Dave Chappelle. Dave was present the day Greg and he were honored with a mural on the wall of Ben's Chili Bowl in Washington, D.C. So many people who were there for the ceremony have passed away: Marion Barry, Jim Vance, and my best friend, Dick Gregory. I had the privilege of presenting Greg as he received his honor that day. Christian and I have gone back to the mural in remembrance of him on his birthday.

Greg liked President Obama's style with humor. He told me both Barack and I would have made good comedians and mentioned that Barack's timing was perfect for comedy. He didn't use that term with mine! While Barack's humor was subtle, mine was much more so, with a slower and deeper voice. Barack's voice has a tendency to use a higher pitch than mine when he is joking and he's more animated. You could easily miss my try at humor because I do seriously dry humor with a lower pitch. So, people often miss what I've said was a joke until I've moved on to something else. I think it comes from people taking what I say so seriously that they often can't easily grasp that I am joking for a while! I rarely raise my voice unless I'm speaking at a rally where there is a large crowd and that's the only way I could be heard. Like Greg, I have spoken before crowds of millions around the world and raising my voice was necessary. That was easy for him, but harder for me. I just always tried to do as Greg said, "Speak so my grandmother could understand me." That meant don't use a whole lot of big words or words in which nobody knew the meaning except you. Some people think that using big words makes them appear smart. I always prefer using words almost anybody can understand.

Dick Gregory with his son Gregory on the day he was painted on the wall at Ben's Chili Bowl June 21, 2017

I was always pleased when I could give Greg ideas for jokes. My ideas generally came from the daily news, as did many of his. In his early days in comedy, the Civil Rights Movement was where he poked fun at some of the silly things racists said or did. While I sometimes suggested jokes for him, he gave me suggestions for speeches and interviews. Since 2016, it seems while political events and statements by many were often unbelievable, many of them were also so silly that they had a bit of humor. He and I made a great team for deciding what we would emphasize in speeches. We never used notes at rallies. It's hard to get a crowd riled up for something if you are reading from notes.

Greg attended nearly every program of the National Congress of Black Women of which I serve as National President and spoke for many of our local chapters in different cities. There were times we were on the same programs elsewhere. Naturally, he didn't leave a lot of time for me, so I tried to speak before he did because he could talk for hours, and nobody complained!

He invited me, and expected me to go to every show that he did in the area in which we lived. He never failed to acknowledge my presence at his shows. He gave my organization, the National Congress of Black Women, a lot of publicity by announcing my presence and saying lots of nice things about me. Occasionally, during a very long program, I had to go to the women's room or just to take a break. If I were gone for too long, inevitably somebody came to find me to say, "He's talking about you," at which time I returned to the room so that he knew nothing was wrong. Often, he talked so long that I just had to leave the room to wake up. Not that his words were boring, but I had heard them so many times, I didn't think I would be missing anything that I had not heard before!

He used some jokes for years, but people never seemed to tire of them. He always mixed the old jokes and bits of wisdom in with new ones. Some of the ones he used often are:

If a man calls me a nigger, he is calling me something I am not. The nigger exists only in his own mind; therefore, his mind is the nigger. I must feel sorry for such a man.

I wouldn't mind paying taxes if I knew they were going to a friendly country.

Last time I was down South I walked into this restaurant, and this white waitress came up to me and said: "We don't serve colored people here." I said, "That's okay, I don't eat colored people. Bring me a whole fried chicken."

For a Black man, there's no difference between the North and the South. In the South, they don't mind how close I get, as long as I don't get too big. In the North, they don't mind how big I get, as long as I don't get too close.

There's a God force inside of you that gives you a will to live. My belief is, you know, certain things have to be explained that's never been explained.

First, feed the people. Hungry people can't listen to the principles of nutrition.

(I have organized *The Dick Gregory Society* to carry on Greg's work and one of our key projects is about food recommendations and distribution. We will also honor other legends for their work.)

Just being a Negro doesn't qualify you to understand the race situation any more than being sick makes you an expert on medicine.

*So why would I want to call myself a conservative after the way
them white racist thugs have used that word to hide behind. They
call themselves new Republicans.*

(I don't really have to wonder because I know what he would say
about Republicans who are silent now after Donald Trump has
been soundly defeated, but the scary part is that nearly half of the
voters in the country voted for him. That's really frightening! I
know he would be using a lot of words that I don't use to describe
all of this chaos that Donald is still creating, but he would be able
to remind us that he warned us back in 2016!)

Until the end of his life, Greg still used jokes and nuggets of
wisdom he told years ago, and they got the same response. No
matter how many times some heard them, they would laugh as
though it was the first time they'd heard the joke or the bits of
wisdom he offered. I've never met a person who knew him and
didn't remember at least one of his jokes or words of wisdom.
Perhaps they told the joke or bungled the message badly, but they
remembered the essence of what he said. He had a talent for using
humor to slice through cultural hypocrisies and racism. He knew
that laughter could help to relieve tension and it often does.

Greg's jokes and words of wisdom still linger. John Legend,
who produced a one-man play about Greg's life called *Turn Me
Loose* said, *"It sounds like he's aware of what's happening now even
though they (his jokes) were written so long ago."*

Greg could joke about Jim Crow laws. He was as funny as he
was courageous. One of his jokes was, *"I waited at the counter of a
white restaurant for eleven years. When they finally integrated, they didn't
have what I wanted."*

He joked about Willie Mays (the baseball legend) who was
often the target of racism, saying, *"You know I still feel sorry for Willie.*

I hate to see any baseball player having trouble. That's a great sport. That is the only sport in the world where a Negro can shake a stick at a white man and it won't start no riot."

He said, *"I went to Ethiopia, and it dawned on me that you can tell a starving, malnourished person because they've got a bloated belly and a bald head. And I realized that if you come through any American airport and see businessmen running through with bloated bellies and bald heads, that's malnutrition, too."*

He had a talent for using humor to slice through cultural hypocrisies and abject racism.

"A Klanner (KKK) is a cat who gets out of bed in the middle of the night and takes his sheet with him."

About Santa Claus, he said, *"I never believed in Santa Claus because I knew no white dude would come into my neighborhood after dark."*

It was not a joke, but about shame, he said, *"I never learned hate at home, or shame. I had to go to school for that."*

This was not a joke either, but his message to young people was, *"Young folks, if you are wise you would talk less and spend more time listening."*

About war, he said, *"The white man sends the Black man to fight the yellow man to protect the country he stole from the red man."* (That was not a joke! Like much of his routine, while you were laughing, he said many serious things that made you think.)

A favorite statement of his to activists that was not a joke was, *"We have something more effective than armies and guns. We have the power of prayer!"*

This one came from a long way back and he so often used it, *"How do you know when you're getting old? It's when someone compliments you on your alligator shoes and you are barefooted!"*

Another one he often used was, *"Segregation was not all bad. Have you ever heard of when there is a collision, Black people in the back of the bus getting injured?"*

Another often-used joke was being asked what he thought about Bob Hope when Bob died and he responded, *"Oh, I thought he'd been dead. No, really, tell Hope's family to get on a plane, go to Chicago to a PUSH meeting and thank Jesse because for forty years he's been running around yelling, 'Keep Hope Alive.'"*

Whenever Greg received an award for his civil and human rights work, he usually accepted it by saying, *"With ten children, I'm so glad I can take something home to the children that they don't eat."*

Another of his oldies he used often was when Lil would ask, *"When are we going to pay Sears and Roebuck?"* His response was, *"You act like we got some money to pay them. When I do get some money, Sears and Roebuck will not be the first thing on my list."*

Aside from the oldies, when Kobe Bryant was accused (never proven) of raping a white woman, *"Kobe came home with a pair of diamond earrings for his wife, Vanessa, but that would never work for a Black woman because she knows that wherever those earrings came from, there was also a matching necklace and a bracelet."*

By the time he finished a show, his conclusion came long after my usual dinnertime. He must have said, "As I leave you" at least a dozen times before he left the stage. There would be long lines waiting to have a word with him, no matter how long it took. I was almost always hungry by the time he stopped talking, but he would hang out with everybody who wanted to have a word with him before we had a chance to leave for lunch or dinner. He never ate what his hosts had prepared. He preferred going to places he knew, and he didn't mind eating the same thing every time he went to one of his favorite places. In most restaurants, attendants already knew what he wanted. He never needed an office because he could go to any major hotel and hold his meetings at the bar or the restaurant. Nobody ever told him the time was up or they needed the table he had commandeered for hours non-stop!

CHAPTER 10

LESSONS OF LOVE

Above all, particularly near the final days of his life, Dick Gregory wanted Black people to be lovable. He wanted us to really care about each other. I can't tell you how many times he reminded us that it is more important to be lovable than it is to be loved. As a result, I can't think of a time I have wanted to hurt someone who'd hurt me because he taught me on so many occasions that our thoughts shape our lives. Sometimes he would stop me in mid-sentence if he thought I was about to express something negative.

At times, he expressed that concept of being lovable so strongly that some might think he was angry as he reminded us, but it was just his way of showing us how urgently important it is to be lovable. It's like all good things in our relations with people would follow if we could just be sure we were not at fault when it came to loving relationships with others. If he had been Secretary of Defense, I don't think we would ever have had a war! The mention of the word defense reminds me of one of his older jokes that he kept in his performances: Upon asking a cousin (he often joked about relatives) to make a sentence with the words defeat, detail, deduct, and defense, the person answered confidently, "Defeet of deduck, went over defence before detail!" That one always got a big laugh.

He expressed his love for everyone by seeing everybody without judgment of who they were or what challenges they were facing. About love, he said, *"Love is man's natural endowment, but he doesn't know how to use it. He refuses to recognize the power of love because of his love of power."*

He reminded me often that it is more important to be lovable than it is to be loved. I still have a hard time with that one with some people, but he said, "There are days when you just have to bow your head, say a prayer, and let things go." No matter how hard that is with some people I know, I do that a lot. Working for a nonprofit, as I do, has to be a labor of love. You make very little money, spend a lot of your own money for the cause, have no retirement or health benefits, and have little time off. Many of those you serve feel they are smarter than you, but never fail to come to you to solve their problems, and some days you question your sanity for continuing. Every time you make an effort to leave, somebody's cause brings you back. Over the many years I have given my all to the National Congress of Black Women. I have had to make things work with some very interesting Board members, many of whom never did anything to advance the organization. On the other hand, a few gave their all.

As Greg walked down a street and saw a person or a group of people, he never failed to stop and acknowledge them. Not just by passing by and waving, but by stopping and asking, "How's your family?" He made everybody seem special. When he encountered people, he made them feel that he already knew them and their family, and that he cared about them as individuals. Sometimes you could see individuals wondering how did he know their family—and most of the time he didn't—but he asked about them anyway!

He would never mind stopping to deal with every question somebody had. Now, that was a bit tricky because once you asked him a question, you were expected to shut up and listen for what might seem like forever until he was ready to end the conversation. He didn't take kindly to anybody interrupting him or disagreeing with the response he was giving you after you asked him something. I learned that had more to do with your not wasting his time. If you asked him a question, he assumed you wanted his unquestioned response, and you had better be prepared to receive what he said!

If you were willing to listen, he had no problem talking with you for hours. He was lovable so long as you listened. He was loved by so many that often when people found they had a critical illness or when one of their loved ones was going through something they couldn't handle, they called him. People considered him to be an expert on everything about health. He never failed them. He always had a suggestion on what they could do immediately before calling up one of his friends who could give them further help. We've driven around all hours of the night to find various concoctions for people's ailments and shipped vitamins to a lot of people all over the place.

It would be difficult to count the number of people he assisted with whatever ailed them. He never failed to have a recommendation. He always thought Black people should love each other enough so that we would be willing to "take a bullet" for them. When he cared about you, I am certain he would have done that for you! Even when he didn't particularly like a Black leader, he tried to find something good about that person that she/he had done that was worthy of praise. I remember how he praised the work of Rev. Al Sharpton when many others criticized him. I was so disappointed when Rev. Sharpton, who seems to make all the celebrity funerals, didn't attend Greg's. I also didn't see him at Cicely Tyson's funeral. I guess he can't make them all!

People came from all over the world, but Rev. Sharpton was not there. I am sure he had a good reason, but we are left not knowing. Rev. William Barber, Rev. Barbara Reynolds, Bill Cosby, Larry O'Donnell, Ed Weinberger, Sidney Miller, Congresswoman Maxine Waters, Dr. Lezli Baskerville, who was there for me every step of the way, and thousands of others did come. He had performed often for the Bronner Brothers programs in Atlanta. One of the brothers attended, and I was so disappointed that he was not allowed to finish his remarks. Obviously, the moderators didn't know his relationship with Greg. He deserved more time. Minister Louis Farrakhan was there in the front row and was one of the speakers.

Speaking of Minister Farrakhan, leader of the Nation of Islam, I remember one day when we were driving by a street with Muslim brothers from the Nation of Islam. It was an extremely hot day. Greg looked at them and pointed one out to me, saying, "Look at that brother. As hot as it is, he's not even sweating. I don't know how they do it. They also never run out of bean pies. They just sell the ones they have and run around the corner somewhere and get more. They always have more!" We'd always stop and buy the latest *Final Call.*

He taught me that it is more important to be lovable than it is to be loved. I have mentioned that statement of his several times because of the importance he gave to it. His advice keeps me grounded and forgiving. One of the more important things I learned from him was, "Before you argue with someone, ask your-self, 'Is this person mentally mature enough to grasp the concept of different perspectives?' If the answer is no, there's no point to arguing with them."

Whenever he walked down the street, brothers, mainly Black men, would walk up to him and greet him as an old and trusted friend. Often, they asked for "a little change." If he didn't have it, he would turn to me and say, "Baby, let me have a couple of dollars." He always thought I had as much money as the bank! He never said no to anybody who asked even if he had to borrow it! He was a big tipper, too, saying that he knew how hard the job of waiting on people in restaurants and bars is—the work of a waiter was difficult. Most were underpaid and deserved more than the average person was willing to tip. So, waiters often did their job with little or no thanks. No matter how much he borrowed, he always remembered to pay it back.

I've seen him sit up for hours answering questions for people who called from all over the world. He never ceased to be able to advise them on what to do or tell them who to call for help and he would tell the person to say that he told them to call. Often, he made the call for them and hooked them up with the appropri-ate person.

He loved helping people. He could *cuss* them out one minute and do whatever he could to help them the next. He was impa-tient with people who asked for his help, then argued with what he advised. Sometimes we'd sit for hours with my reading to him about various subjects and researching various natural treatments and health equipment. He never tired of listening, but sometimes I read for so long that I would have to rub my eyes and prop my lids up to hold my eyes open until we finished a book or articles on what he wanted to know. Other times, when he traveled—even out of the country—he would call at all hours of the night for me to find a passage or a quote from books and articles I had read to him. He often even remembered the page on which the information appeared! He was very attentive whenever I read something to him.

He called for information so often that I could have been called the faxing specialist for him! He didn't use computers or send faxes himself, but he knew that every hotel where he stayed had a fax machine and they knew a lot of information would be coming through for him during his stay. It took him a very long time to agree to carrying a cell phone, but when he could no longer find a telephone booth, because they'd all been taken away, he was forced to get one. He would not use it without the earphones!

He loved people. He loved Dr. Martin Luther King, Jr. He loved Malcolm X. He really loved Medgar Evers like a brother. He loved Michael Jackson, Martin Luther King, III and Nick Cannon as little brothers. He loved Marvin Gaye and was always sorry he couldn't save him. He had dropped Marvin off at his home on the day he was killed and had been scheduled to pick him up the next day to find the help Marvin needed to rid himself of the drug habit he'd developed. It always weighed heavily on him that he was unable to help Marvin on time. He loved Muhammad Ali and told me interesting stories about Ali and several other people. I was sworn to secrecy on some of the stories he told me, and I promised myself I would never tell something that was told to me in secrecy. The success of no book is worth publicizing the secrets I know about so many people. Those stories will go to my grave with me. My word is my bond and whenever I made that promise no one else would ever know if they were waiting for me to tell them. He had friends of all kinds, all religions, all cultures. His feelings about people could be expressed in something Muhammad Ali once said: *"We all have the same God. We just serve him differently. Rivers, lakes, ponds, streams, oceans all have different names, and they all contain truth, expressed in different ways, forms, and times. It doesn't matter whether you're Muslim, a Christian or a Jew. When you believe in God, you should believe that all people are part of one family. If you love God, you can't love only some of his children."* He would tell you in a minute about the Universal God.

At times, there may have been white people who thought that Greg hated them, but that was far from true. He had no problem publicly calling out the bad acts of many. He really had friends of all kinds. He loved and admired many people who were not Black. He particularly liked Mark Twain who wrote the "Adventures of Huckleberry Finn." He was not offended by Twain's use of "Nigger Jim" and said that it was actually a way of acknowledging that Jim had a name. He thought that to be important. He didn't find the use of the word offensive. In fact, he used it as a term of endearment often. I think it was offensive to him only when the person using it meant it to be offensive. That was not the case for Mark Twain.

In his performances, he often said in essence, whenever someone called him *nigger* they were simply advertising his book! His autobiography is called "Nigger" and recently, in addition to the English version, it was printed in Japanese! It's sure to be printed elsewhere in other languages because he had friends and admirers all over the world. On my radio program at WPFW-89.3-FM named *Wake Up and Stay Woke!* that I do in remembrance of him, we are streamed all over the world, and I get calls from many places—from Africa, from Germany, and most from recently Lithuania!

There were others he liked, but there was one white man he loved more than any others. This man was Greg's example of a hero for our cause. He rose above all others. He spoke highly of Ed Weinberger and a few others. They were good friends. However, there was one white man I know he loved and highly respected above all others. That was John Brown. Today and in John's time people called John Brown crazy for taking such dangerous measures to end slavery. Greg honored him for bringing his sons to such a dangerous mission as the event at Harpers Ferry. He said John knew his sons might die and two did die while one escaped. John, of course, was captured, jailed and ultimately hanged for the "crime" of trying to free our ancestors from slavery.

Every year Greg and I went to Harpers Ferry to honor John Brown. We walked through the area from which John conducted the raid. We did a video and discussed the action at the raid. We did it on the coldest day ever with the help of photographer Alvin Jones. We traveled to the jail where John was held. On one occasion, we met one of John's great, great, great (not sure of how many greats!) granddaughters. On each visit, we'd walk to the site where John was hanged. This was a sacred event on numerous occasions. Sometimes, it was the anniversary of the raid. Other times it was the day John was hanged. It was also a way Greg chose to observe his own birthday at times. We taught so many people about the importance of what John Brown had done, and Greg said, "Were it not for John Brown's action, there might never have been a Civil War and our ancestors and we might still be in slavery." For such an unselfish act, he truly loved and honored John Brown. I don't know when the first time was that Greg went to Harpers Ferry, but we were both there for the 150th year anniversary of John's death—and every year thereafter.

Greg was such a caring person. One night, he was downstairs at my place, and I went upstairs to get something. I rarely get sick, but that night I passed out, lying on the floor in agony. While lying there I could hardly raise my voice to call him, but after I had been gone for a long while, he came running up the three flights of stairs. He lifted me up and rushed me to the emergency room at Kaiser Permanente Medical Center. He stayed right there with me until before daybreak when I was pronounced okay. By the time I was released, it was early morning, but he stayed the entire time.

Another time, he was on his way to my place on a Sunday afternoon. He saw many fire trucks near my street and immediately assumed they could be at my place. They were. He parked his car in the middle of the street and ran to my home. As I was watching the destruction the fire was causing to my place—especially to some of my books, with the firemen knocking my windows out, breaking down the gate to my home, drowning my place and wetting what was left of my books—he led me away to a neighbor's home so that I didn't have to stand there and watch as my home was engulfed in flames.

Barack Obama was our President then, and I was often invited to the White House. As a matter of fact, I coaxed Greg into going with me once when he had been reluctant to go to anything there. I believe he thought with all the protests and all the jail stints, he couldn't get through security, but he finally went at my urging. He passed the tests and so many were glad to see him. Mrs. Obama waved to us above the heads of the crowd, as she often did.

The day following the fire, I was due to attend a meeting at the White House without a thing to wear because I couldn't go into my house to get clothing. This was a Sunday night, and I knew no place where I could find something to wear. Imagine my thinking about what I would wear when my home was still burning, but he understood my need to carry on without skipping a beat. He helped me to solve the problem.

He drove me to Virginia where we could look for just any store to be open. We went to a mall and found a Target that was open. I'd never worn anything from Target, but that night I was prepared to wear whatever they had. I had no choice. He had never been inside a Target store and as we walked up and down the aisles looking for something for me to wear, he was amazed by the idea that we could find everything there in that one store that I would need for the next morning. We found makeup, underwear, toothbrush, toothpaste and a suitable outfit for me to wear. He was so proud of me for never skipping a beat with my work, but that is the way I am. He was the same way. He might show up late, but he would get there if he committed to do so!

Unlike him, I was always on time. Like him, I was constantly running from one thing or place to another when we had committed to do something. Doing things just for fun was secondary in both of our lives. We did things out of a sense of duty whether we felt like it or not. It seems we were always running somewhere to get to something for somebody. We even carried signs for various causes in the trunk of our cars, so that we could stop anywhere that we saw some kind of demonstration, find out why they were picketing, demonstrating or protesting, and go back to the car to get the appropriate sign! It could be anti-war, unfair working policies, criminal justice, Occupy Wall Street, mistreatment of Native Americans, women's rights—you name it!

Even though Greg couldn't hear me the night he left this earth, I sat beside his bed and promised him I would carry on the things we always did together. I wasn't sure how, but he had taught me how to try and to believe I could do it. The very next morning, I had to try when I was scheduled to deliver the morning message at church. Somehow, I made it through after opening with a word of his humor and with Chef Daniel Thomas standing in the back of the church coaching me to breathe!

CHAPTER 11

A LIFE OF SERVICE

Greg served in many ways. One was giving advice to people that empowered them and served as lifelong lessons. For instance, Trevor Noah said about him, *"Dick Gregory–a man, a comedian who inspires me to be more, every single day."*

I've seen young comedians and others sit with him for hours, listening to Greg's advice, with some being as nervous as a kid regarding the opportunity to just be around him—to be in his presence!

He did so many things for so many people. He did many speaking engagements and appearances at events and special occasions for people without charging them a penny that made me wonder how he ever paid his bills! He never turned down an invitation from people to help them with their various causes. He attended friends' weddings, graduations, family reunions—you name it! No matter what the occasion was, when he walked in, the occasion became a special one—and whatever people were doing before he arrived, when he walked in the door, the attention turned to him.

He went shopping for vitamins for so many people. He took flowers to many. He never bought just one bunch of flowers. He usually bought them in different colors and took them to people who were ill or just had a special occasion—such as a birthday, an anniversary, Mother's Day, Valentine's Day. Sometimes it was just to tell someone, "You're special." He would go to offices of friends and take flowers to all of the women there.

His civil and human rights trips all over the world were his service to the Movement, to the people who invited him and to our people everywhere. No matter where he traveled, people knew who he was. He courageously went to Iran in an effort to save American hostages. While he was there, he was the only foreigner Ayatollah Khomeini agreed to see.

Meanwhile, as Greg put a pause button on his career in comedy, there was no income back home and many so-called friends began to back away from helping his family since he was gone so long; and I would imagine some were afraid to even be mentioned in the same sentence with Iran. Yet, if he thought an action he took would help, he didn't hesitate to take it. He didn't consider the consequences. He was in Iran for four and a half months. He fasted and his weight went down to 106 pounds. When he traveled to Iran, he was planning to stay just three days, not more than *four months*, but he made the sacrifice anyway. The most time I have been away from home was forty days while on a peace mission regarding the first Gulf War. That was rough— just hanging around in the Arabian Sea not being sure when we would run out of food or when or if we might be able to leave the area alive where our Peace Ship was being held.

In another case, a six-month jail sentence was imposed on both Lil and Greg for their efforts to support Indian fishing rights in the upper Northwest in 1966. Marlon Brandon also went to jail with them, but did not get sentenced to the six months. I guess being white has always had its privileges! Lil was so brave in not bailing out while Greg did so in order to go out and seek support for what they did in other parts of the country. Many people are not aware of the sacrifices she made seeking justice for all people.

Greg was known as a warrior for Native American people, as well as for all of us, and many came to pay their respects for him when he died. He had almost died for the cause of those Native people when he went on a fast until a judge released him because "the judge did not want Greg to die on his watch!"

In yet another case, I traveled with him to Minnesota to picket against the former Washington Redskins in an effort to change the team's name. They were there to play the Minnesota Vikings. Many Native American people were there to honor Greg's presence and to thank him for what he had done years before. We picketed other places where the Washington team was playing. All of those years later, after he and Lil went to jail, going on a fast and almost dying, he never deserted their causes.

He paid for and took food to people in need during the Civil Rights Movement in Mississippi. He shared it with both Black and white people. He considered them all to simply be poor people entrapped by vicious segregation of the races. When people lodged hateful words at him, he responded with humor rather than the same hate thrown at him.

He helped to save people from starvation in Ethiopia with his formula that was a substitute for food. Whenever he ran into Ethiopians anywhere, they remembered and thanked him. Prior to his death, the Ethiopian community in Washington, D.C. came to meet with him in search of a day they could honor him for his kindness. Unfortunately, he left us before the celebration could take place. I hope our Ethiopian friends know how much he appreciated their gesture. It's just that the time to celebrate was never right.

In 2020, as many of us were working our hearts out to be sure we didn't have to endure four more years of a reality show promoter who hadn't a clue what the reality of the Black community was or is, Greg would have told a thing or two to those rappers and the few other Black men who thought they were going to get something from Donald Trump for themselves at the expense of our community. The rappers were not the only ones, but they misled a lot of young Black men to question their need to vote for anybody. These few ignorant rappers (and I don't include the respectful and knowledgeable ones) did a lot of damage with a few young people who didn't vote. Greg would not have hesitated to call them out. I know because I have heard him do that to many traitors to our people, no matter how popular the traitors thought they were. Thank goodness there were many more young people who did vote the right way.

It's not clear how the few Black people who supported Trump could not have known that Trump has never shown any interest in helping our community or in helping anybody but himself, his children and his friends. In saying that, it isn't clear that he really cared about them—especially his so-called friends—because all the way to his last days in the White House, he was throwing his most loyal subjects under the bus!

I don't know how any Black person could miss Trump's angry, vulgar, rambling, insulting rhetoric, along with his more than 30,000 recorded lies he told in his four years living free and at the expense of all of us. In a democracy, truth matters. That's why it was so disgusting that any Black people could allow themselves to be used to try to dilute the power of the Black vote against him, knowing most of us would not be voting for him. Trump caused so much suffering to people of color, Muslim Americans, Jewish Americans, Black Americans, Native Americans, Hispanic people—especially the children, women of all colors and cultures, and so many others.

On the other hand, Trump pardoned and commuted sentences of crooks, while leaving good people who deserved to be pardoned or have their sentences commuted locked up. Under Trump's time in the White House, we've lost allies around the world. We lost so many aspects of the positive change President Barack Obama promoted. It is my prayer that Greg is looking down on us and helping many of us to carry on, to wipe the memory of Donald Trump out of our lives. If he were here, he would be on the frontlines to do just that!

I know he would be reminding us not to get too excited about the current administration and its *Build Back Better* theme, too. He would remind us that if the administration just stopped at the *Build Back* part, the Black community would still see all of the negative things that historically have been heaped upon our community. And unless we stay on top of things reminding, pushing and demanding the third B called *Better* would never happen. No matter who is elected, there has rarely been any progress for the masses of our people without struggle—and even then, the progress never equals that of white people. We still have to work, to remind, and to challenge every new administration. Too often we forget the lesson from Frederick Douglass when he said, "If there is no struggle, there is no progress" and "Power concedes nothing without a demand; it never has, it never will." Others may choose to help in our struggle, but we must lead that struggle. Greg had a way that forced us to listen when he spoke. His style of speaking

sometimes was frantic, always compelling, and he never got tired
of telling us things we needed to know.

CHAPTER 12

REMEMBER THIS—HIS GENEROSITY

Greg often gave his last dollar to somebody in need, never expecting to have the money returned. If he ever borrowed from you, no matter how long it took him to do so, he found a way to return what he had borrowed. He always felt that whatever he had belonged to the Movement, so he never saved or hoarded money for himself. Several people gave him money when he was kind of down on his luck, but instead of using it for personal reasons, he turned it over to the Movement. He never complained. He gave freely and it was as though he was certain wherever what he had, had come from, there was more there when he needed it. Holding onto personal wealth was never a thought for him. He was always eager to give his last to someone in need.

Whenever someone stopped by where he was eating, he invited them to join him if he had finished eating and he made sure the check was on him. Of course, there were times when people walked up to him in the middle of a meal, and he politely asked them to wait until he'd finished eating and he'd be happy to discuss whatever they wanted him to talk about or sign autographs

or take a photograph. Sometimes I look at social media and it's
filled with him taking a photograph with somebody.

He loved buying gifts for people whenever he saw something
that he had heard them mention they'd like to have or when
he was aware of a special occasion in their lives. He believed in
tipping generously for service at restaurants, at hotels or whenever
someone did anything for him. When I asked why he tipped so
much, he told me he remembers the time when he had nothing
and people assisted him. To him, tipping was right up there with
tithing! He always gave more than the tipping sheet called for. It
was always more than 10%! Sometimes his tipping came close to
the entire bill.

He would never mind stopping by somebody's trial, somebody's anniversary, somebody's job promotion, somebody's book
signing, a friend's family funeral, somebody's fundraiser, etc. As
long as the occasion was special for somebody, if at all possible,
he made it important for him to be there.

Like so many Black people, including me, Greg grew up in
poverty and had every reason to grow up hating a lot of things and
people around him, but that isn't the way he was. While he could
easily point out the negatives in the world, he always returned to
love being the answer and being the best way to resolve problems.
If someone around him began saying something negative, he
would caution us by saying, "Don't put it out there." He often told
me about his growing up in the 1930s and what a great challenge
it was to have his wayward dad occasionally visit the home where
his mom, brothers and sisters lived. Those were not pleasant visits
for him. He was always sad when he talked about it.

Just as he and Lil had done when they were younger, Greg
and I selected causes in which we were both interested and would

both be involved—and there were many. I never went with him to an execution of a human being, however. That would have been a bit much for me. He was always there to try to prevent the execution. Of course, I was always ready to be in any other place to picket, to speak or to make my position known. Sometimes it was my personal position; more often than not, I was also representing the organization for which I worked. We spent our own dollars, without pay, to participate in so many causes, both in and out of town. He would give his last dime to help somebody; and when he didn't have it, he knew he could turn to me, and if I had it, I never said no.

THE HOLLYWOOD STAR

Greg never seemed to care about groups honoring him, but that didn't stop Joe Madison, Ted Terry, and Shelia Moses who did the main write-up of Greg's career for the Hollywood Star Committee, and a few other friends who assisted us in putting together the history of his work so that we could submit it for him to receive his long-deserved Hollywood Star. We put out the word and within a few days, friends from all across the country had donated the necessary funds to make it happen. When we ran into several thousand dollars of unexpected expenses afterward that were created by guests and others who were there for the event, I went into my savings account to find the money. He never knew about the money I paid to cover these expenses. I just knew that's what friends are for and he would have done the same for me.

Donations for the bulk of the bills came in from many people who'd never met him but knew about his work and wanted to be a part of the celebration. As he would have wanted it, we made the celebration open. Anyone who wanted to was able to be present. The rapper, T.I., was the largest donor for the star and got our fundraising off to a great start. We appreciated every single dollar just as much as the larger donations. Some actually gave $1.00 and we cheered for that donation just as we did for the larger ones. We didn't have to beg for the money; people from all walks of life seemed to be overjoyed to be able to donate to the star. I met some of the donors during that time and some are still friends today. Eugene Jones, a donor from Oklahoma City, and I still talk from time to time. Recently, he sent me a tee shirt from a Native American designer. The shirt honors women warriors. Among my many tees, it has become one of my favorites.

On the day of the celebration in Hollywood, California, friends came from all over the country. Tommy Davidson, a young comedian from the Washington, D.C. area and I were the speakers. Nick Cannon, Roseanne Barr, Stevie Wonder, Lou Gossett (who was the very first to respond that he planned to attend the ceremony), George Lopez, Rob Schneider, Denise Nicholas, Ed Weinberger, Mark Gallardo, and others were among the numerous guests. Many family members came from St. Louis, Chicago and Washington, D.C. (See www.walkoffame.com for details.) Nick Cannon was a special friend of Greg's who I met at Greg's 80th birthday party and he came down from New York for the occasion.

Lil and several of their children came for the celebration. You would have thought there was something magical about becoming eighty years old. He actually eagerly anticipated reaching that age for several years. He was like a kid eagerly becoming a teenager! A friend, Gwen Moyo, assisted us with making his 75th birthday a special one and I think that every day thereafter, he

looked forward to his 80th! He made that one as well as just weeks
before his 85th.

Even though the final words I heard Greg say on August 19th,
2017, were words he'd been saying all the time, he never once hit
the snooze button on an issue that required attention. He could
talk forever uninterrupted, and nobody ever left the scene. They
wanted to hear every word he said. He never took a break from
the Civil Rights Movement.

The day he left us, he'd been warning everybody in his room
about the problem of doing more talking than acting. There
was just a lot of chattering and laughing going on in his hospital
room. I thought many were too loud, but I didn't want to offend
friends who'd come to see him—never knowing it would be the
last time they would see him alive. Later that Saturday, when so
many people came to see him, I did take the liberty of shepherd-
ing some out of the room into the hallway where they chatted
with each other.

As serious as he often was, he was seriously funny with certain
people. I will never forget the day when he, Art Rocker, and I
left New Orleans to drive to Houston, Texas for picketing British Petroleum. British Petroleum had chosen not to be fair to
the many people its tragic 2011 Oil Spill had damaged. He and
Art Rocker were like two little boys on a playground, hurling
silly insults at each other whether they made sense or not. I kept
putting my hands over my ears, but I could still hear them. What
they were saying was so annoying that I yelled at them to please
give me just a two-minute break. Well, that's about how long the
silence lasted, and they were back at it again.

There was no way to be around him without hearing what he
was serious about, as well as what joke was on his mind. He had a

way of making everybody laugh no matter what. I have seen him
at funerals having people laugh so hard that they forgot the sad
reason for which they were gathered.

Spending so much time with Greg, I began giving him ideas
for jokes. At a certain point, he would tell me that I could be a
comedian because no matter how bad things would be, I, too,
could find something funny that made even him laugh. And he
was the master at finding humor anytime and anyplace. I would
tease him by saying, "Okay, I am going to try that." I began incor-
porating humor in my messages at church and a few other places,
and I got several laughs so I got comfortable using humor.

I was working with many groups on the Equal Rights Amendment, and there was one joke I did that was always requested, as
I was usually the closing speaker of choice at ERA rallies. The
story was about a woman who took her book out on the lake to
her boat and decided to sit back and read on the water. A game
warden came up with his macho attitude and said, "Ma'am, you
can't fish here" to which she answered, "But I am not fishing. I'm
reading." The game warden said, "I know, but you've got all the
equipment here and you could begin fishing at any time, so I am
going to have to give you a citation." She smiled at him and said,
"Okay, and if you do, I am going to have to say that you raped me."
He said, "But I didn't rape you." "I know," she said, "but you've
got all the equipment and you can do it any minute." At that point,
the game warden just said, "Have a nice day Ma'am."

The moral of the story is "Never mess with a smart woman
who knows how to think and read." He loved my contribution to
humor from another version and that I made it my own! He told
me that is what comedians do. They often just hear somebody
else say something similar and they change it to fit their style. He

encouraged me to put that story in my own words and I did. I was able to get laughs on it many times. While I was almost always willing to try his suggestions, I assured him that I would never be able to use some of the language he used to develop his humor. Even when people didn't personally use some of his language, they had side splitting laughs over his use of it. If you ever heard him speak, you know which words I mean.

So, he taught me a lot things, like how to wash dishes properly, how to make hamburgers from veggie mixes to taste like meat burgers, how to make up a bed the way they do it in the military, how to find lost items, how to find a parking space when there was not one in sight, how to do a regular fast, but he also taught me how to do an air fast (That one is tough, but I have done it. You don't even have water!). He also taught me how to hold the venom in my tongue when I really wanted to fire back at something somebody said. (That one wasn't easy either, but I try to do it most of the time.) I admit there are times when people push you beyond your ability to be quiet. He wasn't 100% on that one either. Did you ever try to argue with him or disagree with him about something he was explaining? If so, you know what I am talking about. I never tried to disagree with him, but I have witnessed others trying it and wishing they had not!

Once you asked him a question, it would have been good for you to know his philosophy about arguing with anyone who questioned what he was telling you. It's that one I mentioned earlier, *"Before you argue with someone, ask yourself, 'Is this person mentally mature enough to grasp the concept of different perspectives?' If not, there's no point to argue with them."*

He was always amazed about how I taught him how to crack open a coconut! One day, he decided we should go on a coconut fast. I think we did most of the fasts that existed and if the right one didn't exist, he made one up for the occasion! We went out one Sunday afternoon and bought forty coconuts. That was about all the market had and it was how many the coconut fast called for. We returned to my place and he tried everything he knew to crack open a coconut. Nothing worked. I took the hammer and gave it my best hit. It cracked into many pieces and he was able to eat it. Thereafter, if he ever saw a coconut, he'd say, *"Don't worry about me. I would never mess with you."* He thought it was a miracle how easy it was for me to do it.

For sure, we never failed to be invited to a rally with a cause in which we believed. We participated in so many rallies that we kept placards for various causes in our cars. If we drove down the street and saw somebody picketing, we'd stop and inquire as to what their cause was. It was always something we could support, and we'd excuse ourselves while we went back to the car to get the appropriate sign, return, and we were almost always asked to say a few words. "Few," however, was not a word in Greg's vocabulary, but nobody ever seemed to mind how long he talked for his lectures or his comedy.

I have gone to his events sometime when I got so sleepy while everybody else was hanging onto his every word. I had to go to bed, so I would take a taxi home. Occasionally, by the time I got home, he either showed up or beat me there because he either thought I was upset or he wanted to be sure I got home okay. In either case, he got the message that he'd gone on too long even if others didn't mind his going past the scheduled showtime!

We were speakers at rallies when Trayvon Martin was murdered, when there was the British Petroleum Oil spill, when a district attorney refused to indict someone who'd obviously committed a crime, when a district attorney didn't do the right thing in numerous cases, when a state was threatening to administer a death penalty, when Jordan Davis was murdered and more. We went to Minnesota in the extreme cold of winter on a snowy day when the Washington Football Club (We never referred to them as Redskins) played the Minnesota Vikings at Minnesota. We also picketed at FedEx Stadium when the Washington Football Club played Dallas. We met with Native Americans and supported them to the end. We are not at the end yet, but money talks and when FedEx and Nike spoke recently, the Washington Football Team decided that maybe they could change the name after all even if their owner had said the change would be made over his dead body.

Daniel Snyder, the owner, is still alive, but the team is no longer called *Redskins!* At this time, they have not figured out a new name, but all of our protests have helped to make our point about the unrighteousness of having a team called *Redskins*. God, I wish Greg had still been here when the announcement of ending that horrible name happened. He had spoken out and attended so many events to change the name. I still don't understand why so many people don't get it as to why *Redskins* should be offensive to everybody. Native leaders told the team they would not win much until their name did change. As soon as *Redskins* was dropped from the team's name, they had a pretty good season! Maybe one day, they will go all the way!

When Native Americans were protesting the Dakota Access Pipeline, we were supporters. Greg actually went to South Dakota, but he knew how much I could not tolerate cold, so he advised me to stay in D.C. I found a group, mainly Native American women, protesting in Washington, D.C. and joined them. It at least made me feel better about not going to South Dakota! If the cause was right, one of us was not far away.

We were asked to speak for many rallies protesting the killing of Trayvon Martin. We met Trayvon's mom who attended the same undergraduate school as I did, Grambling State University in Louisiana. Our first major rally regarding Trayvon's tragic killing was on a rainy day on the steps of the D.C. Municipal Building. The second one was in Sanford, Florida where Trayvon was killed.

Next came the murder of Jordan Davis, the son of my sorority sister in Delta Sigma Theta and current Congresswoman, Lucy McBath. Then, there was 12-year-old Tamir Rice, a baby, and it seems the murder of young Black men never stopped. Greg introduced me to Tamir's mom. Greg and I were at events in remembrance of many of them. Since and even during that time, a rash of killings of Black men have continued. There have also been too many Black women needlessly killed, with Breonna Taylor being the latest tragedy.

Greg always spoke lovingly of his wife, Lillian. No matter what he said or where he went, he spoke respectfully and lovingly of Lil. Oh, he had his jokes about her and talked about how they got married while he had no way to take care of her or the baby that was on the way. He would talk a lot about how he met her and how smart she was. He talked about how much he was on the road from the beginning of their marriage. He said he was away performing much of the time while she was raising their children. He felt that it was his duty to be working for justice and said, *"It's not about you and me. It's not about our children. It's about the Movement."* He credited Lil with all the trips to schools and felt that it was not right for him to show up at school when he was at home and have all the attention on him when she was the one who had to go to school for whatever was needed. He said he wanted school officials to know her not just as his spouse, but as the person who was in charge of that division of the family.

He always said he owed his life to Black folks so he responded to every one of their requests that he could. He acknowledged them as the ones who pushed him from the $5.00 people in the nightclubs downtown to places they could not afford, but he always showed his appreciation for the people who gave him his start.

He rarely celebrated any holiday, especially not Thanksgiving and Columbus Day. Columbus Day is observed on October 12th, which is his birthday, so he always claimed it as HIS birthday and said when they were given the day off from school on October 12th, he thought it was because of his birthday! When he left us, he would have been eighty-five slightly less than two months later. My predecessor, Dr. C. DeLores Tucker, died on October 12th, 2005. Upon hearing about that, he asked, *"Why did she have to die on my birthday?"* I don't think she chose the day she would die! On that day, I became National President of the organization she and Congresswoman Shirley Chisholm had built. Half kidding, nothing was supposed to happen on October 12th except HIS birthday!

He was so thoughtful when it came to birthdays and special occasions for his friends. He would spend so much time at the card counter looking for the perfect card for the occasion. I have to say he didn't always judge the cards by the wording. He would select them for the beauty of the card and if the recipients were lucky, the words would be right! Sometimes, he gave me five or more cards for the same occasion. I'm sure he did that with others, too.

As I mentioned before, if we were out anywhere just walking down the street, he would run into any number of brothers who always needed *a dollar.* All they had to say was, "Brother Greg, can you spare a dollar?" If he didn't have it, he never had a problem turning to me saying, *"Girlfriend, let me have $5.00 or $2.00 or whatever."* He always gave them more than they asked for and he always returned what he borrowed.

Whenever we went into a bookstore, which was often, I would look through the books to see if his name was mentioned in any of them. He was almost always there in several books. I found a little book one day and showed it to him. He bought all the books they had that day and gave them away to friends. The book I had found at the Dr. Martin Luther King, Jr. Bookstore in Washington, D.C. across from the MLK statue was called *1,001 People Who Made America.* Not only did he buy out all the books that day, but we went back many times to buy more so he could give them away!

Whenever he bought a book for himself, he always bought one for me. I came to know the reason for that. Whenever he traveled and needed a quote from one of the books, he would call me to read it to him. I have read for him so much that sometimes I had to prop my eyes open to finish a book he wanted me to read for him.

Greg talked about meeting Dr. Alvenia Fulton, one of the greatest nutritionists in the world. She was a natural healer. He said she taught him a lot. She believed in raw food and juices. She believed in healing with cleansing, using herbs, and various natural ingredients. She also believed in fasting. He did a lot of that and I went on several fasts with him. I think we had a fast for every holiday and every cause while others were eating everything imaginable! We celebrated with fasts! When he met Dr. Fulton, he said he didn't know what good nutrition was. He always gave her credit for what he knew about nutrition and that was a lot!

He had a lot of influence on my eating habits! After meeting him, I never took medicine, not even the over-the-counter stuff.

He had a remedy for everything! He was one of Dr. Fulton's true believers. Others, he told me, who were among her true believers were former basketball player Bill Walton, actor Ben Vereen, and singer Roberta Flack.

I just never understood how anyone could eat such healthy food and drink such unhealthy drinks, but it worked for him! He never wanted a small glass of bourbon and Coke. If a server brought him a small glass, he would kindly send her/him back to get a bigger glass. He didn't ask for more whiskey in the glass. There was just something about drinking it from a larger glass that he liked! He would only ask if they would add a bit of Coke, something he never ever advised anybody else to drink. Maybe the bourbon and the Coke neutralized each other!

Greg knew everybody and everybody knew him. He loved Muhammad Ali and talked about some of the funnier things about Ali. He described Muhammad Ali as being in a class by himself. He said Ali was more than a boxer. Ali was often childlike and enjoyed talking. He liked to play games like "Hide and Seek" and he loved children. He would get down on the floor and play with them whenever he had a chance to do so. When Muhammad Ali died, Greg was scheduled to be performing in another place, but in the end, he changed those plans because it was important for him to be in Louisville to say goodbye to his friend. I have since met Ali's business manager, Dr. Abuwi Mahdi, who has told me so much about Ali so I can understand why Greg loved him so much. I have since had the opportunity to visit Ali's childhood home in Louisville, Kentucky.

As I said, Greg knew everybody, and everybody knew him. He introduced me to Cicely Tyson who remained a very good friend and supporter of the National Congress of Black Women until her death. She liked every piece of health equipment we had. She visited many of the natural health people and places as we did. When she was in town, she was often at my place, sometimes spending a week or two. It would be hard for some to believe how personable and humorous she was one on one! Our birthdays were one day apart, and we'd have lots of laughs when she was around. Cicely's birthday was December 19th and mine is December 20th. Every year, she would send me the most beautiful poinsettia that lasted much of the year.

We discovered a Rife machine, and she liked the treatment so much that I purchased one and allowed her to borrow it for a while. Once, on a visit, she took it back to New York with her. Unfortunately, shortly after she returned it to me, there was a fire at my home and the firefighters destroyed it when they broke out my windows and came into my place like Rambo. It was knocked over and all of the glass parts were broken beyond repair. After that, we discovered the bed that I still have. She often used it when she was at my place. She really took care of herself. She even traveled with her own food and juices and when she needed more, we went to Whole Foods or to Mom's. She never deviated from healthy eating habits. She was a very private person, so I won't give details of anything that could be considered personal. Many would be surprised to know that she cooked when she was at my place. When I'd get up, she had already made her breakfast.

Greg introduced me to Stevie Wonder, B.B. King, Kirk Douglas, Martin King III, Dr. Randall Maxey (former President of the National Medical Association), and George O'Hare. While participating in the reading for a play about him, I met Joe Morton, who played Greg in the Emmy Award and multiple NAACP IMAGE Award winning show. Through him, I met Paul Mooney, Trevor Noah, John Legend, Nick Cannon, Dave Chappelle, and the list goes on. I'm proud to say I attended the Joe Morton reading for *Turn Me Loose* in New York and was able to offer several ways for the writer to make the play more realistic in how Greg would have said or done things. However, I didn't think Joe Morton was a believable Dick Gregory, but he was selected to do the part and the show got great reviews.

After Greg left us in 2017, Edwin Lee Gibson did the Gregory role in *Turn Me Loose* at Arena Stage in Washington, D.C. in 2018. I didn't miss a show. I took many friends to see it. Edwin was the perfect actor for the role. He had the right voice, the right build and the right mannerisms. I didn't even have to close my eyes to envision him as Dick Gregory. He not only sounded like Greg, but he looked like him. I had a chance to do the after-show audience participation with Edwin. I was asked a question about what I thought about how Greg would have done a certain scene in the show. Sitting on stage beside Edwin, I hesitated to respond, but Edwin said, "I don't mind. Go ahead," and I did. He was so good in the role that what I was suggesting was minor and only I would know since I was around Greg so much.

People often ask me what I think Greg would have said about certain things. My answer is almost always, "I don't have to think about it. I know what he would have said" because I would already have heard him say it. It was as though he was psychic when it came to telling me about the 2016 election, the chaos that would follow and the calling out of the military and National Guard. Trump's four years happened just as Greg foresaw things. I kept waiting for something like the January 6th riot to happen, knowing Trump was not going without a fight.

FUNERALS AND VOTING RIGHTS

As I said earlier, Greg knew everybody, and everybody knew him. Ron Jenkins, author of *Subversive Laughter–The Liberating Power of Comedy* said the following about him in an autographed book, "With great respect and thanks for the honor of being on the podium with you…" Families expected him to show up at every funeral and major event. As for family funerals, we attended a lot of them. We went to Reggie Toran's relative's funeral in Baltimore. Reggie had been a mutual friend for many years. Greg's remarks made everybody laugh. The burial was to be some distance from the city, so Greg drove behind one of the cars that he thought was going to the burial; unfortunately, that wasn't the case. I don't know where that person was going, but we never got to the burial site. After a long, long drive out of the way, we gave up and worked hard to find our way back to the place where the reception was to be held. That was before we knew about GPS!

We attended a funeral for Keith Silver's relative. That was the first time I had been to a funeral that one could call a funny funeral. Greg told lots of jokes and instead of being about Keith's relative, they were mostly about Keith. Though it was a sad occasion, Keith laughed right along with everybody else.

In 2006, we attended Mrs. Coretta Scott King's funeral in Georgia. It was held at Bernice King's church. I was floored when I heard a decision not to allow Harry Belafonte to attend because of President George W. Bush's objection if he attended the funeral. That seemed out of character for George. He always appeared to be such a happy-go-lucky kind of person. Harry had done so much for the Civil Rights Movement that denying his presence just didn't seem to be right. After the funeral, we drove to Martin King, III's home for a reception. Gwen Moyo was there, and we reconnected after many years. Greg and Martin were very good friends, and he often spoke with him and advised him on important issues. He was like a big brother to Martin. Whenever anyone said anything negative about the King children, Greg stopped them and reminded them about what all of them had gone through as children when their father was killed.

We later attended Yolanda King's funeral the next year in Atlanta. We made a lot of funerals! We attended Mrs. Evelyn Lowery's funeral in Atlanta. Mrs. Lowery was an activist and invited Sheryl Lee Ralph and me to join her in Atlanta to work on a campaign rally for Barack Obama. Her daughter, Yvonne Lowery Kennedy, is a good friend and served on our NCBW Board of Directors until recently. She is also the founding Chairperson of our Birmingham, Alabama chapter. Many of our friends and their family members died within a short period of time, so we went to a lot of funerals!

Greg, a couple of friends and I drove from Washington, D.C. to Georgia to James Brown's funeral. James had died December 25th, 2006. James' funeral was like a rock concert. The night before the funeral, a lot of James' friends came to the hotel where we stayed. I went to bed because I was a bit tired from driving. Greg, on the other hand who never seems to get tired, went downstairs to greet everybody. I had assumed he was in his room and had gone to sleep. After a few hours, he called up to my room and woke me up, saying, "Baby, you've got to come down here. You won't believe these guys." I got up, got dressed and went down to what seemed like a meeting of real gangsters! Most of them, I learned had, in fact, recently been released from prison—and the first place they went was to the James Brown funeral. The conversation was gruesome!

They were loud and bragging about their feats. Their conversation was scary. At least one of them had just gotten out of jail and was doing the gory talk about how he'd been involved in cutting off certain body parts of men that made me flinch! Before I could get back to bed, one of the gentlemen who had lost his voting rights due to a felony conviction asked me to see what I could do to get his voting rights returned in Florida.

Well, he didn't get any satisfaction right away, but I did speak on the issue with the late Congressman John Conyers, and he introduced a bill on the subject. As in other states, in Florida, convicted felons lose their right to vote during their incarceration. Before a certain date, some lost their right for life. Florida ultimately passed Amendment Four where felons can register to vote, but since Governor Ron DeSantis has been in office a requirement similar to a poll tax has been added. The amendment to return voting rights still excluded murder and sex offenses. So, from what I was hearing in that conversation, I don't think those gentlemen will ever have their voting rights returned! Further, over thirty-one states do not allow ex-felons to vote. That is still an unsettled issue that needs addressing. Once a person has paid his/her debt to society, I believe their voting rights should be returned in an effort to start them on their way to becoming or getting back to being a productive citizen.

The next morning, which was the day of the funeral, Greg met and introduced me to a young man dressed in a gold, sequined suit with his hair looking just like James Brown. He was introduced as Young James Brown—so named by James Brown who'd seen his

performance and decided Tony Wilson was so much like him that
the name Young James Brown fit him perfectly. Tony became a
good friend and has been one since that time. He's a great entertainer and he can do anything James Brown could do.

The highlight of the funeral was Michael Jackson's attendance.
People went wild when he walked into the room. The moderator
had to ask for order, reminding people that the occasion was the
celebration of life for James Brown and not a party, but it sure
sounded like the latter! Over the next few days there was a lot of
drama between family and in-laws, but Greg and I managed to
stay out of it. I was surprised because he's usually in the middle
of every issue around him. He didn't even try to referee the James
Brown situation. That was one of many times he advised me to
stay out of it. He knew that I would try to help or mediate in any
situation. He knew I was feeling very bad about how Tomi Rae,
the mother of James' young son, was treated. She and her little boy
were sitting in the front row at the funeral and several men came
up, removed her and the boy and forced them to sit a distance
away. She was also pushed out at the musical part of the service,
but she bogarted her way onto the stage and performed with the
group that included one of James' daughters. I don't know what
their differences were, but I managed to stay out of that too, as
Greg advised.

The drive back to D.C. seemed to be much longer than the
drive to Augusta, Georgia. James was temporarily buried across
from the Georgia state line in South Carolina at his daughter's
place. We didn't get to see that part and I don't know where James
is now, but his funeral was quite a home going service. I just don't
know where his home wound up being!

So much for the funerals we attended! In 2005, Michael Jackson was being tried for allegedly molesting a minor and a whole lot of other charges. The trial was long and took its toll on Michael. He called on Greg to go to California to assist him with his health, so I was able to get a play-by-play report. Greg would call me to find and ship various vitamins to Michael. Ultimately, after a long and grueling trial, Michael was found not guilty. That made Greg very happy because he was very close to Michael. He treated him like a son and often counseled him on various things.

Greg counseled a lot of people, but on the subject of the use of illegal drugs, he would tell the person he couldn't help them because he didn't know what it was like to be a drug addict. He did, however, try to help Christopher Barry through his drug problem. It worked for a while and we tried to help Chris, giving him a job painting the inside of my house. Ultimately, Chris seemed not to be able to accept our help and succumbed to drugs. His mom, Effie, had tried to help him before she passed away, but none of us could help him. Greg and I sat with him all day trying to heal his body, but the baths, the vitamins, the counseling were too little, too late. We were both sad and disappointed.

Greg always tried to make Black women feel good about themselves, to be proud of who we are. He would tell us that Egyptian queens were Black. He said that Liz Taylor was simply playing in a movie when she portrayed Cleopatra, but Black women were the real deal. In all the years I have led the National Congress of Black Women, he only missed one of our annual brunches. Many of the women would surround him after our event and for the next several hours they were still glued to his every word. He was an unabashed feminist before men were called upon to be feminists. He joined women marching down Pennsylvania Avenue in

Washington, D.C.—over 100,000 strong in support of the Equal Rights Amendment back in 1978. He marched with Gloria Steinem, Barbara Mikulski, Betty Friedan, Elizabeth Holtzman, and others. Just like the women who wore all white dresses, he was dapper in his white suit. He was supporting women's issues before I was marching and working for women's rights!

He was always on the go, and often no one knew exactly where he was. To that he would say, *"Jesus left home when he was twelve and didn't return until he was thirty. There's no evidence that Mary went looking for him."* I think that was a message to say he was a free spirit, that he went wherever he wanted to go, whenever he wanted to go, and would return whenever he wanted to do so! That sounds a lot like me, too. We rarely planned anything; things just happened, and we got involved.

Greg was serious about participating in events for his adult children, but he said it was Lil who took care of them when they were growing up because he was gone so often. As his children grew up, three of them lived near him in Washington, D.C. His daughter, Ayanna, is a great entertainer and no matter when or where she was performing—no matter how many times—we went to hear her. If he were out of town for one of her performances, he would ask me to go—and I did. I saw her play, *Daughter of the Struggle*, so many times that I have forgotten how many. She made changes in it often, so each performance was almost like a new play, but the most touching one to me was the one she did after her dad left us. I still go to see her performances as often as possible. She is so creative and such a great entertainer that I don't see why she is not on Broadway!

Toward the end of his life, one or the other of his children would call my house when they didn't know where he was. He was usually at my place. I had a twin bed on the first floor where he walked in. He would either stop there and go fast asleep or run up to the second floor to go to the restroom, then come down and go right to sleep! Even though he had begun to get lost going places, he could always find the way to my house.

He loved Dr. Martin Luther King, Jr. He said that Dr. King made it clear we no longer had to accept second-class citizenship. He described him as fearless, so his courage helped the rest of those involved in the Civil Rights Movement to face the world unafraid. He described Dr. King as a brilliant man with the soul of a country preacher and said Dr. King had a tremendous influence on his life and his commitment to the struggle for human justice.

While he loved Dr. King, Medgar Evers was his ace. Just before Medgar died, Greg said he and Medgar were talking and that Medgar didn't seem disturbed. Yet, Greg said to him, *"Well, it won't be me; it could be you,"* and jokingly added, *"Better you than me."* Not long thereafter, Medgar was killed. Greg's heart was broken because he wasn't there with Medgar. A stage play in honor of Greg was called *Turn Me Loose.* According to him, those were Medgar's last words after being shot.

Greg described Dr. King as a leader. Medgar was that to him, too, but he thought of Medgar as a good friend and a brother. He was a buddy. There were a lot of entertainers he appreciated, but he said, *"Wars and battles are not won by singers and dancers (later he added athletes). They're won by activists. They're won by folks going out there and fighting the good fight to bring about change."* After he died, I know that he would have altered that statement a lot and been pleasantly surprised and pleased about all the things LeBron James and other athletes and entertainers were doing for

social justice and voting rights. I know he was pleased with Colin
Kaepernick's actions.

A PERSONAL SACRIFICE

Greg had a lot of friends who fell into those earlier mentioned
categories. At a certain point in his life, he practically gave up
his comedy, which meant giving up millions of dollars, but he
believed it was necessary for him to be out there putting his life on
the line every day. He still did some of his humor because he said
wit and humor can sometimes disarm the nastiest of intentions
and it did. He used it at his peril before some of the meanest of law
enforcement officials down south. He used it to make a point to
people who might never have gotten the point of how ridiculous
their behavior was.

For instance, one of his often-used stories was about walking
into a restaurant and as he began to order his food, the waitress
said to him, *"We don't serve colored people in here."* He responded
with, *"Good, I don't eat them either. Give me a whole fried chicken."* He
continued the story with the law enforcement officials walking in
to say, *"Whatever you do to that chicken, we're going to do to you."* At
that point, he picked up the chicken and kissed it on its rear end.
He was a true comic genius, but he was so much more.

Never did we go anyplace where someone from different races
and cultures didn't walk up to him and thank him for something
he said or did that they appreciated. Sometimes, they came to
him with the excitement of a kid, reminding him of being in the
audience years ago when they were in college and how what he
said impacted their lives.

The remembrance could have been about something he said
or did regarding the Kent State tragedy, his participation in the

North West Indian fishing case when both he and Mrs. Gregory participated, or helping people in need of food in Mississippi when he rented an airplane and air lifted food to them. There were so many times when he gave his last dollar to the Movement. He felt that was his responsibility and acted accordingly.

He talked about the horrors of crib death and how he was down South with Medgar Evers when he got a call to come home learning his child had died. But for that tragedy, he said he would have been with Medgar the night he was killed in Mississippi.

Many thought that Dr. King was in Selma on the Edmund Pettus Bridge on that horrible day when so many were beaten, including Congressman John Lewis, but he said it was Mrs. Amelia Boynton who was there as the leader. As a matter of fact, he said the Selma Bridge was Amelia's idea and it was Mrs. Boynton who got him involved in the events in Selma. He told me that Dr. King had a tremendous influence on his life and his commitment to the struggle for human justice. Greg gave up a lot to give total commitment to the Movement. Many people made appearances from time to time, but Greg was all in once he became involved.

One of the things that grieved him up to the time of his death about the Movement was Jimmie Lee Jackson being shot five times in the stomach. He was a veteran of the United States military, a deacon in his church and was demonstrating peacefully for voting rights for Black people! That touched Greg greatly. The march was in honor of Jimmie Lee, but his name was often left out as one who sacrificed greatly with his life. It was not just about going from Selma to Montgomery. Greg went there for liberation. We went to visit Jimmie Lee's grave and saw where people had taken several shots at the grave. That was so sad. It made me wonder how people could hate Black people so much, who had done nothing to them, but have done so much to build and protect this country. What good did the shots on Jimmie Lee's grave do for the shooters?

We, too often, choose education over liberation, Greg once told me. He said, *"Liberation means being free–as free as when you came out of your Mother's belly."* He was always proud of the fact that I worked to get a lot of education while using it to work for our liberation. He always applauded Black women who were highly educated and used that education for liberating our people. He never told me what he thought about whether she used her education for liberation, but he would applaud the fact that Dr. Condoleezza Rice, who was prominent in the administrations of George W. and George H.W. Bush, had more degrees than their whole cabinet!

He would make the point that Black men often call Black women strong, and he did not consider that a compliment. White and Black men often call white women beautiful, but not Black women. Too many Black women have been programmed to believe that the Black woman is not beautiful, so she goes to a *beauty shop* instead of to a *hair salon*. To say she is going to a beauty shop, he said is to admit that she is ugly to begin with! Black men have been programmed to believe the same thing. They will refer to their trucks or cars as a beauty but refer to the Black woman as strong. It is as though a Black woman cannot be beautiful and strong, yet most of them are both.

Greg had a lot to say about the word *nigger*. The "N-word," as many used it, is a letter in the alphabet is what Greg always said—nothing more. In referring to the NAACP declaring use of the word nigger was no longer in vogue, he said, *"Not one Black person was sitting in the room when abandoning the word nigger was decided."* He said calling someone the N-word was not a hate crime. *"The word nigger never gave me cancer,"* he said, *"but the pork chop did."* There were some Black people who did not like the fact that he often used the word. It was his way of saying to those who referred to Black people as *niggers, "Sticks and stones might break my bones, but talk won't bother me."* We often joked about taking a *nigger* home with them when we were talking about his book.

Greg often said, *"We might not be able to save this country. It's too far gone."* In the middle of many conversations he would say, *"It's over,"* and *"There is a shift in the wind."* I would wonder what he meant, but now I understand it clearly. Many things have changed, and many are still changing. Even as he was skeptical, he continued to work for the change we desired.

He often said, *"The lowest white person used to say, 'At least, I ain't no nigger.'"* When you think about January 6th, 2021, it doesn't seem that white people can feel they are exempt from being participants in the worst of criminal behavior. Why not? We, Black people, get blamed for everything another Black person does. After Barack Obama proved to be so smart, so qualified (a word many of us came to hate because it's only required to be asked when talking about a Black person), they can't say that anymore. Barack ran white racists crazy the first four years and the next four he did the same and can still do it today!

The guy who followed him to the White House for four years spent his term trying to erase President Obama's name and accomplishments from the face of the earth. Even the most racist person must ask himself, *"Are Black people really smarter than white people?"* I don't know if *all* of us are smarter, but what I do know is that the guy who followed Barack to the White House can't touch

President Obama in intelligence! President Obama and First Lady Michelle Obama were so kind and gracious to Trump after his totally unexpected election, but Trump could not find a way to return the favor to the Bidens.

Greg said once Barack Obama became President, you can't tell a Black child that she/he can't be President anymore because that would be the only kind of President they ever knew. He often said, *"Suppose you have a child when Barack Obama was elected. That child is now eight years old when his term is up and #45 is elected. That child would think, 'I didn't know a white person could be President of the United States.'"* Barack showed those children what a President should be. Trump has definitely shown them what a President should NOT look like!

We traveled to Selma, Alabama in 2015 for the 50th anniversary of Bloody Sunday. That was such a special time to visit. President Obama delivered the remarks to commemorate the occasion. The First Family was there. The George W. Bush Family was there, the late Congressman John Lewis was there, as well as Former First Lady Laura Bush and so many others.

Greg had attended the Selma observance so many times, but the 50th anniversary was really special and not just because President Obama was there, but because First Lady Michelle Obama was there, too! With all the thousands of people who were there, her pause when she got to Greg was seen all over the world. She stopped, hugged him, whispered something in his ear and kissed his hand! I have no doubt that was the highlight of that trip for him. A whole lot of brothers would have given anything to be in his place. While he didn't tell me exactly what she said, it had something to do with how much she admired his work. Again, I don't know one Black man who would not like to have been in his place that day. Even the few Black men I see arguing and supporting the most recent occupant (#45) in the White House (something I fail to understand) drool just thinking about how beautiful, smart and just plain wonderful Michelle is.

I had gotten Greg's ticket from the White House for him to be seated in front of the podium at Selma right in front of all the dignitaries, as well as my ticket and tickets for many other friends. But I never arrived at my seat next to him because I was so busy waiting at the entrance, handing out tickets to people I had invited who were late arriving. So, by the time the ceremony began, I was too far in the back and could not get to my seat. I could only see the screen. Of course, I didn't need to be in my seat to see or appreciate Michelle. I was a guest at the White House the first week they were there in 2009. I met and took a photograph with then Vice-President, now President, Joe Biden.

We found ourselves at the refreshment table at the same time. I picked up a few pieces of cantaloupe. He picked up a sweet roll and upon seeing what I was eating, we moved close to each other and gave each other a hug as he said, "You see, this is why you look like you do and I look like I do!" I think that was a compliment. We chatted for a moment and moved on to mix with others. Since Joe Biden is now President of the United States that photograph is among the most prized possessions in my collection. It reminds me to eat right. I don't know what Joe eats these days, but he certainly reminds us to do what's right!

When I ran into Michelle Obama their first week in the White House, she remembered she had promised to be the speaker for our upcoming tribute to Sojourner Truth where my organization, the National Congress of Black Women (NCBW), made Sojourner the first Black woman to have a memorial in the U.S. Capitol.

Michelle attended the ceremony at the Capitol to do what she had promised and was our keynote speaker. She had come to one of NCBW's brunches and sent videoed messages other times. I had a chance to see her at the White House on many occasions once the family moved in and she always acknowledged me by waving if we were not close together. I STILL WISH I HAD MADE IT TO MY SEAT THAT DAY IN SELMA, but I was glad I had a chance to arrange for Greg to be there. Yes, I would love to have closely witnessed the smile on Greg's face when Michelle whispered something to him! What brother wouldn't have gladly had that kiss on his hand?

Greg always talked about our hating the wrong white people when we hate them. He'd say, *"The white people you are hating couldn't help you if they wanted to."* Of course, he cautioned us against hating or being angry with anybody and about fear, jealousy, and anger. He said these are the things that made us sick, gave us high blood pressure, and all the diseases we often have in the Black community.

He could go and go and go and talk and talk all night as long as he didn't sit down or stop talking. If he did, he would go to sleep immediately. If he woke up and began talking again, he could put that earlier energy back into the conversation and then monopolize the current conversation.

Greg left us August 19th, 2017 and not a day goes by that I don't think of him and miss him. I have pictures of him in so many places in my home and office. As I am working, I can just look up and see him, knowing what he'd be saying to me if I looked tired, sad, or anxious about something. He would not be happy about all the hours I spend at the computer for sure. He always believed in me and inspired me to do things I never thought I could or would do. People often ask me, *"What do you think Mr. Gregory would say?"* about certain things. I can almost always answer, "I don't have to think about it. I know what he would say" because we almost always would have talked about it while he was here. He certainly warned me about all of the chaos around us now (that Hillary Clinton would not win, about Trump becoming President, the White House operations, Trump's unbelievable statements and actions, our challenges with his leaving the White House, the National Guard being called out by him such as during the activities of the Black Lives Matter Movement and more, but not on January 6th, 2021 when they really needed to be called to the Capitol). He foresaw it all. I just didn't understand it would be so bad.

For more than thirty years, we had been good friends and later as best friends. I was known as his running buddy—and did we run! I was glad when we finally switched to walking. I could never keep up with him when he was running. There was a time we would meet each other at 2:00 a.m. and begin our several hours of walking. He would pick me up and we would usually drive to Rock Creek Park. The morning of 9-11, we were in the woods and he stumbled on a heavy vine, fell, and injured his leg. He got up and said, *"Something is wrong. That hasn't happened since I was in high school."*

When we came off the walk that morning, we found that something really was wrong. The airplanes were crashing into the New York buildings, a field in Pennsylvania, and the Pentagon that we could see from my home. He questioned the fact that an airplane crashed into the Pentagon. I must say that no matter how farfetched you thought what he was saying was, he was usually right. He believed it was some kind of missile. No one has ever shown us any parts of the airplane that crashed into the Pentagon. He always asked where the parts of the airplane were if that happened. We had a friend whose daughter died at the Pentagon that day. Whatever hit the Pentagon, as in the other places, the whole day was a tragedy.

ARRESTED FOR THE CAUSE

We went everywhere together. We went to Senegal for the African/ African American Summit. We went to Jena, Louisiana to help get the young men out of jail who were wrongly incarcerated. We protested in all kinds of weather and in so many places together for certain causes, but most of the time I was told to follow orders from the police and back off so I could get him and others out of jail afterwards. Greg, Martin King, III, Ben Jealous, George Clooney, George's dad, Nicole Lee of Trans Africa, and I went to jail over the horrendous things going on in the Sudan. I was one of the last to get the handcuffs on. By the time we arrived at the police station, I had been able to work my hands out of them. I was afraid not to have them on when the police came around to take us into the station, so I put them back on! Nicole Lee and I were the only two females arrested and would have become stir crazy if we had stayed in the cell a minute longer. We had just a small cell, approximately 5x7 foot with a little hole, and had to take turns looking out to see what was going on.

The men were brought into the station after Nicole and I were taken inside. When George Clooney was called up to be searched, the police had him raise his hands and for some reason the officer told him to lift his foot. Looking through our little hole, we could see George was doing a friendly resistance. We saw the bottom of his once white socks. He said, *"If I knew you were going to do this,*

I would have worn clean socks!" All of the men were photographed and taken to a cell nearby where they could see each other, and we could hear Greg telling them jokes. They were having a great time. Nicole and I were suffering in the cellblock. I had never been arrested before. I had only been in jail cells to get people out and I could leave whenever I wanted to, but not that day!

There was another time he was arrested while I was out of town and he went on a silent strike until I returned. It was during the Christmas holidays and I was in Louisiana visiting my mom. I was away for several days, but when I got back, I learned he was at the main D.C. jail and they were bringing him over to D.C. Superior Court for his hearing. I was told he had been assigned a court appointed lawyer, but when I arrived the lawyer told me he was refusing to talk to her. I went back to the cell and his court appointed lawyer asked me, *"Is he crazy?"* since he wouldn't talk to her. I relieved her of duty on his behalf. Poor woman. She'd apparently never heard of Dick Gregory!

Back in the cellblock many lawyers were standing around his cell talking about him, when they met him, where, etc. because he was talking to no one there. I had absolutely no time to prepare to go before the judge and, fortunately, I didn't have to. When we were called into the courtroom, the judge came in, was amused when he saw who the defendant was, then asked the prosecutor and me to introduce ourselves. After we did, the judge took over, and spoke directly to the prosecutor. He asked, *"Young man, do you know who this gentleman is?"* The prosecutor said, *"Yes, your honor. His name is Richard Gregory."* The judge said something like, *"You don't really know him, but let me tell you who he is."*

The judge proceeded to say in years the order of events happening:

1. He was involved in the Civil Rights Movement and was arrested many times where the cases were dismissed every time.

2. He worked to assist Indians with their fishing rights; he was arrested but the case was ultimately dismissed.

He named a long list of times when Greg was arrested, and the cases were dismissed. And finally, he said that all of those cases were dismissed. *"And today, this case is dismissed."* The judge never asked for any of the details the prosecutor had obviously planned to present. I assume the judge had already read the charges. At any rate, I didn't have to do any work that day!

Another time we went to court ready to defend him. For that time, I had really prepared. The judge was a woman we had never known or appeared before, so we were uncertain what she would do. She didn't look all that friendly, so I was a bit nervous. She walked in and asked if we were ready. I answered *"Yes, Your Honor."* She asked the government the same question. The government answered her question saying, *"No, Your Honor. We are requesting a continuance."* She said, *"You mean you are not ready? THIS CASE IS DISMISSED!"* I could never get to practice law with Greg because the cases were always dismissed!

I tried to defend him once more in Landlord/Tenant Court. I found some point in the law that showed the Landlord had not followed the procedures for the things charged to him. Again, the case was dismissed! He was always getting into "Good Trouble," so I remained one of Dick Gregory's lawyers who never lost a case because I never had to explain anything! I never had to put up a defense!

CHAPTER 13

GREG'S DRIVING

Whenever I would mention Greg driving somewhere, most people could not believe he knew how to drive, since others were always picking him up and driving him to and from an airport somewhere. The few months before he left us, I noticed he was beginning to forget how to get places, so I often went with him to ensure that he got there.

I will never forget the day we were driving south on I-95 from Washington, D.C., going to a seminar in Virginia. Some person from abroad was speaking that evening. On the ride, I looked down for a minute and when I looked back up, he was very close to the exit where we should have gotten off the freeway. I told him so, but he refused to take the exit. He never liked to be told to make a quick exit, but that was the only way I could let him know how I thought we should get to the event.

As I was trying to figure out what we should do, other than drive the long distance back to the exit we missed, he made an exit which I was not familiar with and wound up in a large complex where all of the apartments looked alike! I had no idea where we were—not even what town we were in since there were no signs around. He simply stopped the car and waited for me to figure out what to do to get back on track. That was before either of us had a GPS. Not knowing where we were and I no longer saw the freeway, I just kept guessing and saying turn here, turn there, etc. This thing called woman's intuition finally got us where we had been trying to go. Several hours later, after stopping at every service station or convenience store on a pretty lonely highway, we finally arrived at what we thought was our destination.

The trip normally should have taken an hour or less, but here we were at the address where there were no apartments as had been described to us. So we parked and called the host. The apartments were far off the beaten path. After total frustration from trying to find the place, someone walked out to where we were to get us. From there we had to walk about a quarter of a mile before we arrived.

Now getting back home was another adventure since we were obviously returning without going back the miles out of the way when we had arrived at the place—and it was now dark! As we were coming up to a toll station, I told him he needed to slow down because we had to pay the toll. I've learned that men don't like for you to tell them how to drive. So, whether that was the case or he didn't hear me, he drove right through the toll stop without pausing and nearly hit a car. He blamed the other car for getting in his way. I thought he still should have slowed down to try to avoid an accident, but that never crossed his mind. It was one of those moments when he had suddenly decided he was right, and he was going to stick to his guns no matter what. I was breathing deeply and vowing never to ride outside D.C. at night with him again if I didn't know how to get there. I pretty much said my last rites on that trip. Just in case we didn't make it home without an

accident, I called his son, Christian, and told him what was going
on. But we finally arrived at my place. That was one of those, "Oh,
what a relief it is!" moments.

When Greg's memory got pretty bad and he was getting lost
more often, he never forgot how to get to my home. So, whenever he left his home without informing his children, one of them
would call to ask if I had seen him. Usually, he was at my place.
He had taught me shortcuts to my house from various places, so
he knew the way from many angles!

I promised that if we got home safely that night, I would never
go out of Washington, D.C. with him again! (Of course, I didn't
keep that promise, but finding our way was easier after that.) He
was not the greatest or safest driver. After all, being a celebrity,
people had been driving him around most of his life. I have seen
him stop at a light or stop sign and go to sleep while he was pausing
for the right of way or for the light to change. On our last trip out
of the D.C. city limits, he was determined to get a television for my
birthday, and the place he wanted to get it was near a restaurant
in Maryland. That's all he knew; the place where he wanted to get
it was near a restaurant he had once visited. He didn't remember
the name of the restaurant or the street it was on. I drove on that
trip and after a couple of hours we actually found the place with
him calling the shots on every turn! The traffic was vicious as it
always was on a Friday evening, but we ultimately found the place
and made it back to D.C. safely.

There was another interesting trip with him driving. We were
going to visit Dr. Louis Freidli in Emmitsburg, Maryland. Well,
first of all, I had never heard of Dr. Freidli or Emmitsburg, but
Greg had a way of finding natural health doctors, vitamins, books
and health equipment. We left Washington, D.C. about 3:00

p.m. one day, drove past Hagerstown, MD in the rain towards Emmitsburg that was only about a two-hour trip under normal circumstances. Cars were bumper to bumper, and it was raining. I guess Greg's bumper was too close to the car in front of us and my right knee took the brunt of the bump when he hit his brakes. I was limping around for a few days, but we soldiered on through the rain and a lot of mountains that I have since learned were not on the route we should have taken. We took the very long way to Emmitsburg! Instead of the two hours it should have taken us, we arrived about 9:00 p.m. that night. Fortunately, the good doctor had patiently waited for us. Every trip had its interesting surprises!

CHAPTER 14

GREG AND THE MOVIES

Greg loved movies. Often, he'd see the same movie eight or ten times. He would take friends he thought should see the movie. He would drain every bit of knowledge he saw in a movie and he would explain it to anybody who would listen. He didn't miss a beat. He saw things in movies that I never saw, but I only went one time to see a movie. Once I went with him to see a really violent movie and had to leave the theater to sit in the hallway until he finished seeing it. He would go so many times to get every ounce of meaning out of a movie. Sometimes those meanings seemed farfetched, but at some point, the meaning he'd offered became clear. He could see things in a movie that nobody else saw. Sometimes, he would explain to me how movies predicted the future.

The last movie we saw together was *Black Panther*. That was one of those WOW movies and I did go back to see it after he was gone. I took our mutual friend, Art Rocker, who came from Florida on business related to what Greg, he, and I had worked on with British Petroleum. No movie seemed to match the movie *Django* for Greg, where Jamie Foxx did a masterful job. If for no other reason, he loved that movie because a Black man gave a white man the beating of his life. He offered little or no other reason for liking that movie so much. Of course, I agree that the guy deserved the beating.

I think Lil liked movies, too, as much as he did. (I called her husband "Mr. Gregory" on most occasions. I always called her "Mrs. Gregory," but she finally insisted that I call her "Lil.") She seems to have seen every movie he saw, but maybe not as many times as he did. The moment he walked out of a movie he would call her to discuss it with her. The conversation was always long. I just walked around the lobby of the theater nearby until he told her everything he saw in the movie. I think she mostly listened because, as usual, I could hear his enthusiasm in telling her about the movie.

Greg appeared in several movies during the time I knew him, so I received a play-by-play explanation while the movies were in the making. I heard everything about the last movie he made about Buddy Bolden, a prominent Black musician. He spent much of one summer down South making that film.

CHAPTER 15

LIL AND HIS SCHEDULE

Lil ran Greg's schedule, so he called her many times a day no matter what was going on. Nobody dared commit him to do anything without going through Lil. I learned that early on when many of the people who saw us together frequently thought they could get me to commit to his doing something for them. I was instructed to just refer them to Lil, and he was in touch with her throughout the day.

Greg carried a lot of coins until he had a real problem calling home so often or calling anyone when all the telephone booths were removed. He had no intention of getting a cell phone, but he was ultimately forced to get one because he was not going to stop calling people! It was years before he would agree to get a cell phone because he did not believe it was good for our health to have one around your body all the time. Out of necessity, he finally had to get one because when you were away from home there was no other way to make or get a call or to communicate about anything. Public telephones just magically disappeared once cell phones came into being. He still would not put the cell phone up to his ear. He always used earphones. I have not yet learned to use earphones. No matter what I do with them, they just don't seem to work for me. Once he faced the fact that telephone booths were not coming back, he made the adjustment to call people with the cell phone. He rarely answered his cell when others called him. It was specifically for him to call people when he wanted to talk with them!

One year I was blessed to make The HistoryMakers. My neighbor, Amy Billingsley, knew that Greg was a friend and appealed to me to get him to do the interview. She said she had tried to get him to sit down and do the interview for quite a while but was unsuccessful. Amy is a very good friend, so I told him he should do it. We called Lil who scheduled it and he did the interview. Amy and Julieanna Richardson at The HistoryMakers had to quickly put the team together over the weekend and find a camera person for the interview on a Sunday before he changed his mind. The equipment was set up in my living room and it went very well. He actually sat down for the whole interview without taking a break. He didn't complain about having to be still for so long. He talked from about 6:00 p.m. to 1:00 a.m., telling many historical facts! Once he got in the groove, he just kept going and provided them with a lot of information.

CHAPTER 16

THE CELEBRITY GOLF CLASSIC

In the fall of 2016, as NCBW celebrated its 32nd anniversary, we decided to do something we had not done for a few years, but we intended to carry it on for years. We wanted to have an event for NCBW members who stayed in Washington for a few days beyond the Sunday brunch. We organized a golf tournament and asked Greg to allow us to call it the Dick Gregory Celebrity Golf Classic benefitting our Young Ambassadors' program. The planning went well with only a few glitches. The day planned for it didn't cooperate. It poured down rain, so we had to postpone it. Because of that, we lost a lot of the players who had stayed over immediately following the brunch.

Ultimately, we had it several weeks later, but it was a bit much for Greg. The weather didn't cooperate then either and it was very cold. He told me, "I don't know a thing about golf, and it just doesn't seem right for me to be the sponsor." That was the end of what we had hoped would be an annual event. Nevertheless, I have photos with the words "Dick Gregory Celebrity Golf Classic" to prove he headlined at least one! Everybody who participated was just glad to have him there. They didn't care that he knew nothing about golf! From the beginning, Christian almost vetoed it and I think it was the only time we ever had an argument! He's been an angel about everything since that time.

After the Classic, Greg convinced me that he didn't want to do that anymore and naturally, I didn't ask him again. Because of the rain and cold weather, I agreed with him that golf shouldn't be played at that time of year, anyway. I regretted having expected him to participate, and by that I mean just to show up; he was just there to entertain people who had come. He didn't go near the golf course! A woman by the name of Karen McRae had talked me into asking him to headline our event. Soon thereafter she disappeared after I learned she had figured out how to, without authorization, charge a whole lot of her personal debts to my credit cards and to our organization.

Finding out I was reluctant to report a Black woman to the police, Greg "ordered" me to go to the nearest police station and report her because it was learned that she had done this to several other people previously. The police took the report, assured me she would be prosecuted, and they continued to tell me that for several years each time I asked for a status report on the case. They told me about her record of doing this kind of thing to others, and that she had served time and been on probation for many years from those crimes.

Nevertheless, the Metropolitan Washington, D.C. Police Department that would have handled what Karen did under Federal statutes did not prosecute her as promised and never informed me of that decision until I called. They gave no reason other than they turned the matter over to the District of Columbia's Attorney General. I never heard from them, however. We took the loss because of potential legal costs and I worked to try to make up for the deficit. Our organization had no funds to pursue the matter further. Had Greg still been living, I know he would have lectured me about trusting people and about trying to help certain people, then he would have assisted me in finding legal fees. Her actions wrecked my credit because my name was on all of the credit cards she used. Ms. McRae got lucky. Because of all the damage she did to our treasury and to my personal credit we had no funds at the time to pursue the case. I have since raised funds to keep my organization and me from going bankrupt!

CHAPTER 17

GREG THE PROPHET

I mentioned Greg being prophetic. He always seemed to know things ahead of the rest of us. In 2015, I was so excited about the very real possibility of finally having a woman President. Nothing said to me Hillary Clinton would not be our President. I was so sure. In my excitement, he stopped me in my tracks one day saying, *"I know you are all excited about the Clinton campaign, and I hate to disappoint you, but she is not going to win. After the campaign is over, there will be chaos. The National Guard will be called out. There will be chaos and a problem getting Trump out of the White House."* He was right. Trump did everything possible to hold onto the title of President, including inciting thugs to break into the Capitol and do a lot of damage, while threatening to kill various people, including his own Vice-President!

As of the 2020 election, almost everything Greg said then had already happened. Donald Trump began making his case for calling the election a fraud before it was over and he began filing silly lawsuits in numerous states. With someone who was on record as having over 25,000 lies, no one took him seriously except maybe Donald Trump, Jr. and Rudy Giuliani! Most Republicans were afraid to disagree with him, so most of them just kept quiet. The courts certainly didn't agree that Trump had won anything! Every case he filed, he lost.

The day after the Inauguration in 2016, thousands of people—mostly women—descended on the National Mall and all around it. No matter how much you wanted to get to an open space, you couldn't do it. I think even some of the women who had voted for Trump had a change of heart that day. Before that day, it was clear to me that I was in triple trouble—once as a woman, again as a Black person, and finally as a Progressive human being. It was a very orderly protest and there was enough evidence the Russians had at least tried to interfere in that election. Most of us could not imagine Trump winning the Presidency!

When Greg would talk to me about how bad things were going to be under Trump, for once I almost closed my ears so I could not hear anymore. I didn't even want to hear anything he was saying about our future under Donald Trump. It was too scary to think about. What he was saying just couldn't be true. To be sure, I didn't believe it at the time he was warning us. Well, it looks like he knew what he was talking about—as usual. I heard many people on the news talking about the great possibility of Trump not voluntarily leaving the White House if he lost the race to Vice-President Joe Biden. Even Trump began using language that he might not leave as all Presidents before him had done. He just kept saying he'd won when the evidence was not on his side. This sounds a lot like the chaos Greg had mentioned years before. After the election, I had come to believe many of what others called conspiracy theories. I believed the Russians had interfered in our previous election. I believed Hillary Clinton had actually won. I believed Donald Trump knew exactly what was going on to steal the election from Hillary, but never did that make any of us want to go and tear up the Capitol while making threats on people's lives and actually taking the life of some.

I had heard Greg talk often about "a shift in the wind" and I didn't know exactly what he meant. But, since he's been gone, and we came into the Black Lives Matter Movement, the shift became clear. I had seen so much of what he said come true. Whenever he heard someone mention MAGA or *Make America Great Again*, he would always say, *"You act like America was once great for all of us,"* meaning for Black people. Like we are seeing now with so many others, Greg survived many of the same things Congressman John Lewis and Dr. C.T. Vivian and others survived. No matter how bad or how brutal things got, these men just kept on pushing and wound up living long lives to see many things change. Yet, nothing thus far has perfected our Union for us.

We are still fighting to be treated fairly—to be allowed equal opportunity. Yes, America has a lot of promise, but so many are just fine with enjoying their white privilege and not disturbing what is. No matter how many Black friends they claim to have, they are satisfied with having things the way they are for fear they will lose something. Despite that, during the height of the Black Lives Matter Movement, I saw a lot of promise for change when so many non-Black people participated in those marches. The other problem we face as Black people is having too many Black people looking for personal approval of whites or hoping to grease their own palms by being willing to sell their souls for personal gain at the expense of the masses of Black people. I won't name them, for they know who they are, and I think most of us know who they are. They will get angry at my statement because they know who I am talking about.

When the 2020 Presidential election ended, Joe Biden was declared the winner and Donald Trump was the loser. It's an understatement to say that Trump didn't take that too well. He declared himself the winner by a landslide, despite the fact that he'd lost by several million votes! I so wish Greg had been here on January 6th, 2021, the day Biden was finally declared the winner by the Electoral College. He would have said, *"I told you so,"* meaning he had told me about the chaos Trump would cause; just as predicted, he did that.

Trump urged his supporters to come to Washington and attend a big rally near the White House. Thousands stormed the U.S. Capitol and ran roughshod through the building, destroying things and chasing Members of Congress from their session to confirm the election of Mr. Biden. In the process, lives were endangered—and as a matter of fact five people, including a police officer, died that day—and police officers were found to have participated in the rioting. We learned later that two others died that day. The sight of the police officer being battered and squeezed mercilessly by the mob, screaming for his life, was almost unbearable. Black policewoman, Captain Carneysha Mendoza, was squeezed between doors and almost had her arm broken by rioters.

As world leaders witnessed what was going on, many appeared to be in shock. For all the good that many had said about American democracy, even leaders of other nations were horrified. I don't have to wonder what Greg would have said. He certainly would not have been shocked. He would have pointed out the obvious by saying something like, *"You act like white people were always decent. Your memory is short if you don't remember what they did to the Indians, to Black people during slavery, to the Vietnamese and to countless others around the world.*" He, no doubt, would have expressed that in saltier language, but he certainly would not have been surprised by what the thugs did that day.

I know Greg would not have been surprised by the rioting on Wednesday, January 6th, 2021, when supposed "patriots" overran the United States Capitol—actions incited by no less than Donald Trump, Rudy Giuliani, and Donald Trump, Jr. Trump's friend, Mike Lindell, the useless My Pillow guy (whose pillow is just as useless) egged Trump on at the White House in the days following the riot, as did his on again-off again buddy, Senator Lindsey Graham, who wiped his hands of Trump one day and a few days later supported him. He had a chance to fly on the airplane with Trump a few days after the riot. They weren't the only ones who showed their colors.

There were shocking numbers of people supporting Trump when his actions had wrecked the Capitol, killed and injured people, and left the reputation of our nation in shambles. As if that were not enough, we heard one after another Congresspersons talk about their fear of being assassinated for voting for the second impeachment of Trump. After all Mike Pence did to cover up or remain silent about harmful actions to the American people, Trump didn't even inquire about him or send in help to rescue him that day of rioting at the Capitol. I am sure Greg would have said that Pence got just what he deserved for always going along with Trump's dangerous behavior. I can't even think of descriptions for Josh Hawley, Jim Jordan, Ron Johnson, and countless others.

CHAPTER 18

WHAT FRIENDS ARE STILL SAYING

I knew I would always remember Greg, but when WPFW-89.3 FM radio in Washington, D.C. invited me to do a program, I chose to use the words I had last heard him say. That statement had a lot of meaning for me when I chose as my theme song, "Wake Up Everybody."

Some of the people I have interviewed on the show are:

- Otis Williams who is the founder of the Temptations. He was highly complimentary about Greg, but who wasn't?
- Joe Coleman and the group Leonard, Coleman, and Blunt (LCB). They came from very popular groups like the Temptations and the Platters. Their comments were very complimentary of Greg's talent and his humor.
- Gloria Dulan Wilson. She is a Delta Soror and good friend who often co-hosts *Wake Up and Stay Woke!* with me. She always has a Dick Gregory story when she is on the program.
- Joe Simon. He gave a personal story about them riding around Chicago in a limousine together and having a great time. After Greg left us, Joe (who is a Bishop now) and I worked on an online Voter Registration project. Because of COVID-

19 people were afraid to go out to register. The election for which we were registering people proved to be well in need of the voters who wanted to register. We helped them to register, and Lord knows we needed their vote! We didn't match Stacey Abrams, but we needed every vote to take us out of the past four years we had just experienced. Currently, Bishop Simon and I are working on another voter registration drive and the restoration of a school in Joe's hometown of Simmesport, Louisiana which is near my hometown of Alexandria, Louisiana.

- Dr. Robert Turner, Pastor of Vernon AME Church in Tulsa, Oklahoma. When I asked if he knew Dick Gregory or remembered anything he ever said or did, he responded with a time Greg was on a radio interview. He said, "I love Dick Gregory. He was one of the best comics—Black or white—of all times." He came from a generation where entertainers were engaged in the community. He recalled the time he heard Greg on the radio and a woman was trying to get him to talk about something—about how we can succeed, about how we can overcome a racist system.

After Greg explained a few things we could do, she kept pushing him to tell her more. At that point he asked her, "When America went to the moon, did they go on a radio show and tell everything about what they did or had to do?" He told her, "You shouldn't tell all of your plan on a radio show, but there is a plan." He went on to say this as he scolded her as to why we can't broadcast everything we do and how we plan to do it. All of my guests knew Dick Gregory. All of them had something they could say about him even if they'd never personally met him.

Dr. E. Faye Williams' broadcast of "Wake Up and Stay Woke!" on Justice lineup at WPFW-FM 89.3 (8/15/2018)

My nephew, Ronald Troy Smith, did meet Greg and was around him often as his trips to my office and my home were frequent. Once when he and Greg were in Philadelphia at the same time, he'd just been asked if he were going to an event to which Greg was also going. Troy thought that going sounded good, but he didn't have a ticket. Well, shortly thereafter, he ran into Greg on the street, who said to him, *"Let's walk over here."* Ironically, this was a ticketed event. Someone came out to get Greg (who never needed tickets to get in any place) and Troy was able to go into the event. He saw that being with Greg, he didn't need a ticket. I had that same experience many times. I went places with Greg often, but I only had a chance to get him into the White House once without his having a ticket! On another occasion, Troy said he went to a movie and was sitting at the top of the theater when he spotted Greg in a lower row. That was not unusual because he often went to the movies, and frequently he went alone—even many times seeing the same movie.

It was not unusual for Greg to sleep through much of the movie. I would nudge him a lot, hoping that would keep him from having to return to see it so many times. I don't think my efforts helped because he often returned many times. Troy said he went down and spoke with him. He said, *"That was an incredible movie, wasn't it?"* Troy said he agreed that the movie was the real deal. He was then asked if he wanted to see another movie. It was already late at night, but Troy said he agreed, so they just went back downstairs to get tickets for another movie. They didn't get out of that movie until 3:00 a.m.! That was not unusual either because Greg never slept by the clock or because it was late. He just slept whenever he was actually sleepy. The time didn't matter.

Other nephews met him: Keith Wallace, Terrence Scott, David and Darryl Oden. A lot of my nieces met him, and they all loved and admired him. My brother, Sonny, and several of my sisters met him. He always took the time to make them feel special and whenever he was in their towns, he invited them to his shows. My sister, Siv and her husband Al went when he was in Houston. He never failed to call and invite them. My sister, Gussie, met him when we went to the demonstration in Jena. He'd met my mother several years before the rest of the family did, and he always called her Mother and asked about her. He also met my sister Marie and her late husband Rudy Copeland, who was also an entertainer. He went to shows with me to see my sister, Bettye LaVette, and he loved her talent.

Through the years I met all of his children, but I knew Ayanna and Christian more than the others. His children were pretty scattered across the country, but I always heard from him what they were doing and how they were. Everyone who has children should hope they would be like Ayanna and Christian. They are so talented in different ways and both have that same ability as their dad to make people smile.

As I mentioned before, I had heard Greg talk about a good friend, Cheryl Smith in Dallas, Texas, but I'd never met her. When I met her, it was obvious she was that friend. After Greg died, we became good friends, and she has been on my radio show. She also has a newspaper in Dallas and I have been in her paper several times. She told me she'd met Greg in 1995 when she emceed a program where he was the speaker. Little did she know that he would become such a special friend who she adored and respected. She said he pretty much became a regular on her radio show at KKDA-AM in Dallas. He went to Dallas almost every year to participate in a celebrity bowl-a-thon that she held to raise funds for scholarships. Out of about twenty-three bowl-a-thons, he attended about twenty-one, and she said he never touched a bowling ball! That sounds just like the golf tournament! He never played.

She told me, however, when he was in town, he visited schools, the county jail, Black businesses, Dallas' only HBCU - Paul Quinn College, museums, and Black-owned bookstores. She said as time went by, she came to know and love him and his beautiful wife, Lil, and over the years with him she visited his daughter, Ayanna, at her job. Anytime she needed medical advice or she was visiting the D.C. area, she had to connect with Christian, too, Greg's son who is a chiropractor. When she came on my show at WPFW, she talked about Greg's work ethic and his extensive knowledge on so many topics. She thought it was amazing how they would have talks about all types of issues and he always made himself available. Whether she called him about her fibroid tumors, job decisions, family, or just to say hello, he showed her love. She told me she still gets angry at times because his death was so significant, as was his life. He gave so much to so many. She said she became a better person because of him. Not only did he make her laugh, but he helped her to understand the importance of a smile and he helped her to become more lovable. Naturally, I could agree with her because I felt the same way. After he died, she wrapped his pictures around her newspaper, so that it looked like a monument to him!

My good friend and fellow counselor, Johnny Barnes, was also on my show. He once bailed me out on a legal case with an incorrigible client who reminds me of Donald Trump. The client thought he could just tell me what to say to the judge and that was proof of the point he wanted me to make on his behalf. I couldn't get him to understand that's not the way the law works. Johnny came in to help me when I was about ready to give up on the client. Johnny once said, "Dick Gregory carried us on his shoulders during a time in the saga of this Nation. He was the first Black person to run for President." Johnny's daughter, Sia Tiambi, recently joined him on a tour of the National Museum of African American History and Culture, which, among much else, bears an exhibit in tribute to Greg. While tickets are hard to get, they are worth pursuing, as this edifice properly captures important moments and eras in America's muddied Black History. Young people especially should go to visit the museum.

Julieanna Richardson, Founder/CEO of The HistoryMakers, was on "Wake Up and Stay Woke!" Before I was able to get Greg to do The HistoryMakers interview, she said she had tried for years to get him to do it to no avail. When he finally agreed, she said they weren't really prepared. They had to rush to find a photographer on a Sunday! She said it was well worth the scramble!

Special showing of Dick Gregory for family and friends at the National Museum of African American History and Culture (Pictured with Dr. E. Faye Williams on 4/17/2017)

Tony Wilson (professionally known as Young James Brown) told me about the time he first met Greg. It was on a movie set of *The Wiz* in the 1980s. "Upon seeing him I told him I was a stand in for Michael Jackson. He appeared totally unimpressed, and told me without skipping a beat, 'Well, stand your a** over there!' Greg was chatting with comedian Nipsey Russell (The Tin Man).

While he was chatting and directing traffic in the area, his mission there was to see about Michael Jackson's health scare issues. Again, during my last concert at the Promontory in Hyde Park (IL), Mr. Gregory called me up to the stage to chat with him as he does when I'm present where he is performing. First, knowing that I knew her, he asked me, 'You talked to Faye?' I replied that I had, to which he said, 'Well, tell her you were here.' He then just said, 'Do a flip'—which I did onstage right in front of him. He knew I could do just about everything on stage that James Brown—the Godfather—could do. I also did just what else he told me to do! I told Faye I was there, but I call her Queen Angel!"

CHAPTER 19

CAUSES HE TRULY CARED ABOUT

Now that we've seen what others thought about Greg, let's turn the table and talk about someone he greatly admired. It was an understatement to say that Greg loved and had great admiration for John Brown. In 2015 on a freezing cold day, we went to Harpers Ferry to do a video on Mr. Brown. We walked all over the area where John Brown, his sons and others had fought a battle for our liberation.

On the day he was hanged he said, "I believe that to have interfered as I have done, as I have always freely admitted I have done on behalf of despised poor slaves, I did nothing wrong, but right." He had done this attack to encourage enslaved people to run away from their masters and gain their freedom. Greg admired him for taking his own sons to battle. He was passionate about ending slavery. The attack ended badly for John Brown, but the fact that he sacrificed so much for us made him one of Greg's true heroes. We had the honor of meeting one of John Brown's great, great, great granddaughters. Not sure if I have enough greats there, but you get the idea.

At WPFW radio, the year after Greg left this earth, we did a Dick Gregory Walk in remembrance of him on his birthday. Edwin Gibson, the actor who played him in *Turn Me Loose* at Arena Stage in Washington, D.C. and I did the walk together. We started out early and finished before everybody else. At that time, I had never done a 5K, but it turned out to be easy. I later began walking five miles per day with ease. I still do a couple of things he always insisted upon: drinking water and walking. Those were always among the things he cared about.

These days, Black women are getting the same treatment by police as Black men. When young Breonna Taylor was killed in Kentucky, I wanted to go on the fast as Greg would have done with young Vincent Gonzales the moment he announced his fast. I made the mistake of asking a few friends if they would support me in doing so. I was disappointed when all of them advised me against doing it. If Greg would have been here, I would have consulted him and I am sure I would have done it anyway no matter what anyone else said; but, during the COVID-19 virus I agreed the risk was too great without having someone to monitor my fast.

I was honored to serve with Dr. Ben Chavis and Rev. Willie Wilson as Co-Chairs of the 1995 *Million Man March*. That was such a busy period in my life that I didn't see Greg very much during the planning for the March, but on the day of the March he was there. He knew I would be speaking so he came down to the launching area to let me know he was there.

One day, we flew to Houston, Texas, stopped at the Occupy Rally that was going on all over the country. We had stopped by many of the rallies in different cities. We spoke for the rally in Houston, then rented a car and drove out to an Indian Reservation for a big celebration they were having. As we walked around the Reservation, I saw a buffalo live for the first time. I remember our hosts treating us like royalty. They didn't know me, so they must have accepted me as a friend because of Greg! We stayed overnight after the celebration and drove back to my sister, Siv's and her husband Al's, home in Houston.

One Sunday, we drove to upstate New York where he was to speak for an event. We went in a direction that I am sure was out of the way, far out of the way, but I had learned that even when you knew the best way to get someplace, you never tell a man how to get there! I had been yelled at a few times about giving a man driving directions (not by him; he welcomed help with directions, but I didn't really know where we were going!), I was just along for the ride. We were late, very late, but it was a pleasant drive. When we finally arrived, the people there were just glad to see Greg and they were so ready to hear whatever he was prepared to say. They were serious fans.

He did a show in New York City called *On the Great White Way*. Keith Silver and I went up to see it. Greg's daughter, Lynne, came. We got souvenir tee shirts that both advertised the show and had the famous Dick Gregory protocol for losing weight on the back. Instructions called for dozens of vitamins and I took every single one of them! I still wear my shirt that, at this time, has a few holes in certain places, but I wear it all over the place—and I never fail to get compliments on it and people asking where I got it. I have never seen anybody else with one like it. I still have a sweatshirt that I got when I went to his place in Ft. Walton Beach years earlier.

Almost any day that I open my mail, I have a photo or a message regarding somebody who took a picture with Greg or went some place to hear him speak and what a difference he made in their lives. I get news articles and comments in books about him. Through my radio program, through my weekly articles, and having heard us at rallies and various programs where we spoke, people still remember him. Christian often fills in for me on my program in honor of his dad, so we are both easy to find and we often get pictures, books, and other memorabilia in remembrance of Greg. Many people just want somebody to know they, too, knew him. Many share stories with us about him. Christian gets items of remembrance from people and we share our collections! We've received gifts from as far away as Lithuania! We get calls from people who just want to tell their Dick Gregory story and we always welcome them.

When Cathy Hughes was transitioning out of doing a daily radio program, she would call to ask me to fill in for her often as guest host. I never had a problem with finding a guest for the hours I was on air. If Greg called, nobody else had a chance. It became the *Dick Gregory Show*. He had also been a regular with Cathy Hughes, owner of the station. There was never a shortage of things to talk about when he was around. He always dominated the conversation. I didn't even have to prepare for the show because whatever he wanted to talk about became the subject of the discussion! He could be in Spain or any other place in the world, but he always called in and had something to say. He sort of became my unofficial co-host whenever I was on!

At one time he served on the Community Board of Directors at WPFW 89.3 FM. I asked him how he kept up with all the issues they were covering. He said, "I didn't. I would just look at how Marion (Barry) was voting, and I would vote the same way!" He and Marion had worked in the Civil Rights Movement together and they were very good friends. Both were members of Alpha Phi Alpha Fraternity, but that is not what drew them together. It was more about what they both did during the Movement and their genuine concern about poor and disenfranchised people. At one time I worked for Marion—and what a ride that was! Linda Greene, a friend I succeeded as Chief of Staff and I became his everything while there! He had done so much good for so many people, so we felt that taking care of him was our duty. Greg often stopped by the office and we always welcomed his advice.

THE N-WORD

I write for *Trice Edney Wire Service* which distributes my articles to Black newspapers in the country. One day, like Greg, I got really frustrated with Black and white people whispering and saying the *N-Word*, knowing they meant *nigger*. No racist ever called Black people the *N-Word*. I decided to say what it is in one of my articles. If you're a Black person, I don't care how much money you have, where you live or work, who your non-Black friends are, whether you attended Harvard or Howard, whether you have dark skin or light skin, to those nearly one half of the population who supported Donald Trump and any number of his cronies who are Senators, Governors, House Members, state and local officials, you're still a *nigger*.

I didn't intend to say the *"N-word"* ever again. People don't call you the *N-word*. They call you just what they're thinking. We must stop acting like saying the *N-word* somehow softens the blow of what racists mean when they call you *nigger*. Whichever paper prints my article and chooses to put n.... r, or calls it the *N-Word* that's on them, because after meeting Greg, I have never called it the *N-word*. Calling a person the *N-Word* is not a crime; but, calling someone *nigger* with an insulting or illegal intent could be. Why should we protect someone from being prosecuted who disrespects us with hate words? Besides, use of the word *nigger* sold a lot of books for him. They still sell today. He would say, many people are happy to take a *Nigger* (the book) home with them! Recently his book was printed in Japanese. I guess he has friends in Japan!

As I watched all the accolades about Congressman John Lewis and various remembrances of the Civil Rights Movement, I was reminded of how much Greg wanted us to remember that Jimmie Lee Jackson gave his life for our voting rights. He was a veteran who served in defense of our country, but that didn't matter to the racists who were doing everything they could to deny people like Mr. Jackson the right to vote, so they beat John and they killed Jimmie Lee.

On February 18th, 1965, while Mr. Jackson was out peacefully protesting for the right to vote in Alabama, he was shot and beaten while unarmed by state troopers and he died eight days later. All he was doing was trying to gain voting rights for all of us. He was a church deacon, peaceful protester, and civil rights activist in Marion, Alabama. Greg was concerned that Mr. Jackson didn't always get his rightful credit while other names were so often in the news. I had a chance to visit Mr. Jackson's grave while on a trip to Alabama with the Evelyn Lowery Annual Tour Group. I was shown gunshot dents on his grave put there by people who still hate other human beings for no reason other than the color of their skin.

Greg said it was Mr. Jackson's death that inspired the Selma to Montgomery March that continues today. He would also give credit to Mrs. Amelia Boynton Robinson who was the first person to invite him to Selma for the events and the annual marches that later became known as Bloody Sunday. She was a leader of the Civil Rights Movement in Selma. The Selma to Montgomery marches began shortly after Jimmie Lee was killed on March 7th, 1965. About 600 people participated. That number has now grown to thousands who show up at the same time each year. Before the year was over, the Voting Rights Act of 1965 was signed by President Lyndon Johnson. It was always surprising that a President from the South would be the one to sign it.

Greg taught me the importance of the marches across the Edmund Pettus Bridge. I went for the first time in 2014. I was honored to be a speaker at a women's program in Selma, invited by Yvonne Lowery Kennedy who was Chair of the National Congress of Black Women's chapter in Birmingham. The program was held in the George Wallace Auditorium. I must say in order to go into that building, I had to pretend it was named for George Wallace the Black comic!

Greg and I went to Selma again for the 2015 Selma to Montgomery March when President Barack Obama was the speaker for the 50th Anniversary. Greg had been in Selma fifty years earlier so this was a special occasion for him seeing a Black First Lady, her daughters Sasha and Malia, and our Black President, after all they had gone through. Like so many of us, he was so proud of this President while recognizing the limitations under which he served. I returned to Selma a year later and was invited to speak at the historic Brown Chapel for an afternoon rally. I had been the speaker for a program sponsored by the women the year before.

Greg told me of his having gone to Selma in 1963 where he spoke for two hours (that was short for him!) before the "Freedom Day" voter registration drive. He never left the Civil Rights Movement. He practiced its principles religiously. He gave so much money to the cause of freedom, as well as his time. He explained the Movement to others, and he got all of his friends involved to some extent. I was no different. Living on the West Coast, I had only one chance to participate in a march with Dr. Martin Luther King, Jr. I later participated in many rallies for various causes with Greg (peace/anti-war, justice, voting rights, women's rights, workers' rights, Native American causes, DACA students' issues, anti-gun rallies, etc.) He gave up everything he had for the Movement—but he always felt blessed.

Greg had a white friend by the name of George O'Hare. As a result of things Greg (and Rev. Jesse Jackson) taught him, George became active in The Movement. He wound up naming himself "A Recovering Racist" and wrote a book called *Confessions of a Recovering Racist* about his introduction to and experiences in civil and human rights. George was the President/Founder and CEO of the Recovering Racist Club and he named Greg to be Chairman of the Advisory Board. They had membership cards made and gave them to people they thought were worthy of belonging.

The famous Father George Clement was on the Advisory Board. Father Clement's input was to have St. Francis Assisi's word on their letterhead. It read, *"Lord make me an instrument of your peace. Where there is hatred, let me bring love. Where there is doubt, let me instill faith. Where there is darkness, let me bring light. Where there is sadness, let me bring joy. Oh, Divine Master, Grant that I may not so much seek to be understood as to understand, to be consoled as to console, to be loved as to love. For it is in giving that we receive, it is in pardoning that we are pardoned, and it is in dying that we are born into everlasting life."* Often, Greg reminded me that it is more important to be lovable than to be loved. That was one of his constant teachings. I try always to practice that, but some days and with some people, being lovable is really, really hard! Sometimes there are people in your life who make you want to return fire with fire, but Greg taught me not to do that!

While reminiscing about his first meeting with Dick Gregory, Father George recalled him as slightly overweight (later in life, it was hard to imagine Greg ever being overweight, but he was!) and one who smoked like a chimney—one cigarette after another. By the time I met Greg, he wouldn't go near a cigarette which was a good thing because I would not have been able to bear being around him. George said Greg's jokes showed white people the absurdity of their racist mindsets. He described Greg as brilliant, exceptional, and a man who knew something about everything under the sun. George's description is just about the way I would come to describe him. He knew everybody and everybody knew him.

A lot of people have talked about all the money Greg lost when he pretty much turned his life over to the Civil Rights Movement and stopped doing his comedy. He missed out on millions of dollars, but he never seemed to worry about that. He did what he felt compelled to do. While I didn't go through as much danger as he did, I've had my share. I ran for the U.S. Congress in Louisiana and that was not a piece of cake. I was constantly threatened just for running for office and for talking about issues that normally were not discussed in Louisiana politics.

I've been escorted out of town, for my own safety, by law enforcement personnel that I wasn't sure I could trust. I've had sharpshooters station themselves on buildings while I was speaking in open areas. I've had the aircraft in which I was flying from one place to another forced down at gun point, and surrounded by armed police and army personnel carriers that were not there to support me, but to do harm. Yet, I have never felt that my story came close to the dangerous situations in which Greg willingly went into, places like Alabama and Mississippi, knowing he could be killed like his friend Medgar Evers. He went time after time anyway. He also spent a lot of time in Louisiana in an effort to run drug dealers out. I had the privilege of marching with him there, even though I didn't really know him well at that time. I was just pleased with what he was doing and wanted to be a part of his efforts.

Greg gave so much to so many causes and expected nothing in return. Years ago, he had a formula called 4X. It was what he took when he ran across country. He used it for both energy and nourishment. He sent tons of the formula to Ethiopia after a severe drought. That formula saved thousands of people. Whenever we went out and saw Ethiopians, they remembered him and thanked him. They wanted to honor him, but as many times as they asked, they never had a chance to confirm a date and before one could be arranged, he passed away. His formula helped many. It helped Michael Jackson's brother who was badly injured in a car accident. He said that it helped the Pittsburgh Pirates. Some say that it gave them the energy to win a World Championship! I personally knew many of the Pirates and I remember what a great team they were. Willie Stargell, Bob Veale, and Al McBean were friends. They were leading members of the team during those great years for the Pirates and when they played in Los Angeles, many of the guys came to my home for dinner. I always attended their games and their coach called me their good luck charm because they won so often when they played in Los Angeles.

No one would ever be able to question the validity of Greg's Black Card, so when he not only sent tons of food to Mississippi and to Ethiopia, he also sent 300 tons to white Appalachians! I don't think it occurred to them to turn the food down because it was donated by a Black man.

He had a lot of friends everywhere. He lost many friends when they were young, and he still talked about many who preceded him in death. He loved Malcolm. Days before Malcolm was killed, Malcolm had invited Greg to the mosque in New York for a big program they were having. Greg turned down Malcolm's invitation and said, "Man, they are going to kill you, and I am not going to let them get two of us for one." He didn't go and, of course, his friend Malcolm was killed.

Another time when Marvin Gaye was having his challenges with drugs, Greg took him home one Sunday. They talked about Marvin's problem and Greg got him to agree to get treatment for it. He dropped Marvin off at home with a promise to pick him up the next day to take him for treatment. Unfortunately, tragedy struck later that Sunday. Marvin was killed in a tragic family dispute. It grieved him that he never had a chance to get the help for Marvin that he needed, but he tried.

He had regrets for not being able to get help for Christopher Barry, Marion Barry's son. Chris's mom, Effie, called Greg to try to help him get the drugs out of his system. Greg invited me to go with him to Effie's place. Greg purchased loads of vitamins and used other methods to clean up Chris' system. It worked for a while, but after Chris' mom and dad died, he went back to his old habits and that cost him his life, though not because Greg had not tried hard to help him.

Greg had so many friends. He introduced me to many of them. When some had already died before I met them, he made me know more about them and who they really were. A few I already knew

and became greater friends with them. Among the many I met or
learned more about from him were Medgar Evers, Rob Schnei-
der, Muhammad Ali, Ed Weinberger, Marion Barry, Malcolm
X, John Bellamy, Jim Kelly, Dr. Randall Maxey, Mark Gallardo,
Martin King, III, Art Rocker, Dr. Jynona Norwood, Cheryl Smith,
Andy Shallal, Nick Cannon, Dave Chappelle, Michael Jackson,
John Legend, Jennifer Holliday, Bonnie Marshall, Sidney Miller,
George Clooney, Lou Gossett, George O'Hare, Juanita Britton
(AKA *Busy Bee*), Speaker Nancy Pelosi (he told me of serving
in the military with her brother), Kathleen Kennedy (daughter
of Robert Kennedy), Rev. Horace Sheffield, Trevor Noah, Joe
Morgan, Marvin Gaye, Michael Douglas, Leslie Uggams, Tracey
Ross, Stevie Wonder, Mary Wilson, Paul Mooney, Cicely Tyson,
Lynn Whitfield, Dr. Glenn Ellis, Wanda Sykes, Lillian Cosby, and
the list goes on and on! A lot of young comedians credited Greg
with helping them, or they just admired him for the ground he
broke for them.

Chuck Brown, known in Washington, D.C. as the "Godfather of Go-Go," died in May of 2012. Much like Greg, he got his
start shining shoes. Two of his more famous customers were Louis
Jordan and Hank Williams—neither of which did the kind of
music Chuck Brown did. Greg and I went to his celebrity funeral
at the Howard Theater. Chuck's big hit was *Bustin Loose*. He was
the pride of Washington, D.C. and all of D.C. seemed to love
Go-Go music.

It also seemed that all of D.C. was there to say goodbye to
Chuck. I went with Greg to pay our respects, too. Someone came
to us on that pretty warm day to get us through the line faster, but
we stayed with everyone else trying to get in. I never liked cutting
in front of others who had been standing in line just as long as I

had. The same was true for him. We rarely accepted invitations to cut the line as it's called when you get a chance to go around someone who was closer to the door than you were. It doesn't matter who you are, you should not be able to get in front of someone who was there before you. If Greg was on the program, he might accept the invitation to move up, but usually there was another door through which performers entered.

We went to many events at the Howard Theater, including many of his performances. We went to see Young James Brown, Bettye LaVette and others. The really sad time we had when we went there as I remember was when we went to hear B.B. King. By that time, B.B.'s memory was just about gone. We were both near tears as we saw staff take his microphone, then his guitar, then lift him up from his chair and lead him off the stage against his will. Instead of singing that night, he mostly talked, kind of rambling.

It is so unreal that Greg is dead—a word that is still hard for me to say when talking about him. Some of the things of which he always said that I will never forget are as follows: *"I never learned hate at home. I had to go to school for that."* If you have read his book *Nigger* or the book he did with Robert Lipsyte named *An Autobiography by Dick Gregory with Robert Lipsyte,* you will find the haunting story as to how that statement came about and I pray that any teacher who reads Greg's story would never do that to a student. My heart breaks every time I read that story of his teacher cruelly embarrassing him in class.

Another important part of his philosophy is, *"One of the things I keep learning is that the secret of being happy is doing things for other people."* I have many opportunities to do that, and I think he would be proud to know what I do every time I have the opportunity to do good for somebody—often people I don't know or people who come to me for help because they knew I was a Dick Gregory disciple and would know how and be willing to help them. I always try.

I have heard him say many things, but my favorite is *"Leave the world a better place and people in better shape than you found them."* I try to live that part of his philosophy every day of my life. In fact, I have made it my own philosophy and God has blessed me with many opportunities to help others find their way through some of the most difficult challenges. Perhaps the recipients of my help have felt better, and I am very sure helping others has brought me great joy.

Just after my best friend died, those who knew us best and all the work we did together to help others urged me to carry on Greg's work—something I had already promised him I would do on the night he left us. One of the first things I did was use my weekly column to offer advice on actions all of us could take in order to get people involved in making changes to better their lives. Second, I accepted the invitation to become a host on WPFW-FM 89.3 and I could think of no better name for the show than "Wake Up and Stay Woke!" With that show, I try to give people an opportunity to express what they are thinking about certain things going on in our world and talk about how they plan to make a difference, as Greg always did. In addition to the radio program, I established *The Dick Gregory Society* as one way of carrying on his work. I have chosen Father's Day of 2021 to make it a permanent observance in remembrance of him and other legends. He was like a father to so many. Additionally, I have established *The Dick Gregory Society* as an instrument for doing my very best to not only carry on the kind of work Greg did, but to encourage others to do even bigger and better things. That is what he would have wanted. He always talked about building on things people before us designed or created and the responsibility we had to do that.

Usually, shortly after we see actions we don't like, we express our dissatisfaction for a moment, maybe even take an action, and soon after forget about the problem with which we were faced. You might say, we wake up for a moment, then go back to sleep. Because problems continue to occur—especially for the poor, the disenfranchised, people of color—we must stay woke if America is ever going to form that more perfect union for all of us. It takes our active involvement—not just our complaints. Like Greg, I never get tired of being an activist, and I'm disappointed when making a difference that matters is beyond what I am capable of making happen.

Dick Gregory often said, "The Movement"—meaning the Civil Rights Movement—taught him to wake up. He never veered from the direction the Movement took him and he was able to march through danger and through meanness and hatred, but he did so without hatred. You would know when he didn't like things, but he never showed hatred. He would say, "Meanness won't destroy white people (meaning those who are racists); it destroys you, so don't do it." He would say further, "It's not about love; it's about can you be lovable?" He lectured everybody who would listen to refrain from hate, fear, jealousy, and anger. He talked about how these things harmed the doer, not the one you meant it to hurt. He had so much wisdom and he spoke in terms my grandmother could understand. I use that phrase whenever I hear someone speaking in terms that are difficult to understand. I was known as his running buddy and I miss him every day and I remember so many of his teachings. I live by as many as I can. I just can't use some of the language he often did, but he understood that and would have been shocked if he heard me use some of his words! I always got the point, but sometimes you would think we spoke a different language!

Dick Gregory and "Sonny" (Dr. E. Faye Williams' brother)

Greg and my brother Vernon Williams, Jr., known as "Sonny," were good friends. Here they are sitting in my living room in Washington, D.C. I remember our riding together in Louisiana to go to the town of Jena to represent young men who were being unfairly treated for things that happened in high school. My brother was a much-loved Louisiana Deputy Sheriff. Like Greg, he drove very slowly. It seemed that I was the only one in a hurry to get to Jena, but we finally did arrive. I will never forget the night

Greg arrived in Alexandria for the Jena rally and walked into the meeting hall where Michael Baisden and many who were in town to go to Jena were gathered. There was bedlam. Everybody wanted to talk with Greg or just touch him, something that went on throughout the protest in Jena.

After the Jena event, my brother had a stroke and later came to live with me in Washington so that I would try to find better health care for him, and so that I could assist in his recovery plan. He lived with me for a year and I did my best. He lost the weight he needed to lose on doctor's orders. He reunited with Greg and they had great times together, but then Sonny's wife back in Louisiana died. He returned home where he ultimately died not long after that. It was tough because I lost both Greg and Sonny so close together.

So many people I talk with have a fond remembrance of the Bahamian Diet. Recently, Kenneth Simpson (former Grambling University and professional basketball player) told me he once had dozens of cans of Greg's Bahamian Diet stored in his grandmother's basement. I told him I wish he still had those cans because I know so many who would love to have the formula back. John Bellamy, a mutual friend of mine and Greg's, has put together a formula that does the same thing the Bahamian Diet did and more. The new formula is called *The Caribbean Shake for Optimal Health*. It's on the market now at Amazon (bit.ly/caribbeanshake) The former Bahamian Diet users as well as new users will love this one! Greg was still with us when the Caribbean Shake was first announced, but left us before it went on the market. His product helped so many people with their weight and general health issues that I wish he could be here to see what this product will do, simply because it was first identified with Greg. So many people believed in him and followed his advice on health. Learning so much about the dangers of pre-existing conditions through this COVID-19, he would have been speaking about it and convincing people of the need to take better care of their health. That's what he did daily when he was with us. If he were here and he would be asked what he would do about the vaccine to guard against the coronavirus, while he wasn't all in favor of medicines, he probably would have joked as his friend Reggie Toran reminded me, about how he would have gotten Black people to get the vaccine by saying, "Just put some barbecue sauce on it!"

At one time, Greg would run for miles no matter what the weather was like. Finally, I began to see him switch to walking. We would walk and talk before day in the morning. Even though he called it walking, his pace was so fast that I could hardly keep up. It was not until he'd left us that I began appreciating walking all alone. Some days, I remember him as I walk up to five and a half miles regularly. I have now mellowed down to about three miles per day in the summer. But in the winter I can still do five! As much as neither Greg nor I liked cold weather, we could still walk longer and farther in the cold than we ever could in the heat. We even walked in the snow. I must confess that on rainy days, I do much of my walking on the trampoline! I'm not much in favor of walking and being out in the rain.

Greg would have loved Barack Obama's new "semiradical approach" in his speaking at Congressman John Lewis' funeral. He would have loved the new Barack who is out there every day working to help us elect his old Buddy, Joe Biden—something at which he was successful. He kept quiet once he was out of the White House and gave Donald Trump more than the space he deserved, but the "orange man," as many called him, continued to

disrespect his predecessor while he did absolutely nothing important after nearly four years in the White House, other than try to
tear down any and everything he perceived as having been done
by Barack. While Barack has been respectfully quiet for nearly
four years, Trump kept chipping away at Barack's accomplishments and saying weird, but untrue things about Barack. In the
closing days of the 2020 Presidential election, Barack returned
the fire, and his rallies brought out a whole lot of Black voters who
might have otherwise stayed home. Like Barack, Kamala Harris
being on the ticket energized many Black people—especially Black
women—and to our overwhelming joy, both Kamala and Joe were
elected in 2020.

NOW IT'S YOUR TURN

Greg also would have loved Congressman Lewis' final statement
that was revealed the day he was buried when he said, *"Though I
may not be here with you, I urge you to answer the highest calling of your
heart...I have done all I can to demonstrate that the way of peace, the way
of love and nonviolence is the more excellent way. Now it is your turn to let
freedom ring."* All of his life, it was clear what Greg would want his
many mentees and followers to do once he was gone. It's our fault
if we weren't ready. You see, most of us could not conceive of Greg
ever dying. The night he left us, people from many places called
to confirm his death because they just could not believe what they
were hearing on the news about his being gone.

He was so respectful of his fellow Civil Rights leaders. He
would stop what he was doing any day to respond to their requests
to appear with them for various causes. Actually, he would do that
for any program if he believed in their cause. He once jokingly said,
(I think he was joking) that he spoke at a PETA meeting where they

served steak! Of course, he never ate at these banquets no matter what they served. He had no problem leaving a banquet to go to another place of his choice for dinner. As long as the restaurant had mashed potatoes, fried okra, turnip bottoms, or deviled eggs, he was satisfied. If the restaurant had sweet tea (lots of it), that was like a banquet for him! He would put mayonnaise on everything—not just a little bit, but a whole lot. I guess you could say that was his one sin with food. Count butter in there, too! The few food items he consumed almost always went better with a tall glass of bourbon and Coke until near the end of his life when he stopped drinking anything other than water and sweet tea—many, many glasses of sweet tea with far too much sugar! Other than sweet tea, he hardly ever touched sweets, but he could drink glass after glass of sweet tea. He drank so much of it that shortly after drinking several tall glasses of it, he was off to the men's room—often rushing to get there. After driving along and drinking his tea or water, his first step at my place was usually rushing off to the restroom before speaking! So often, he had to do the pee dance to successfully get to the restroom on time! Everybody knew him for drinking lots of water. Beverlye Neal, as did many others, told me they learned to drink lots of water from him when he was often on WOL—Radio One talking about the value of water.

CHAPTER 20

HE LOVED AND SHARED INFORMATION

On any Sunday, one could find Greg at a bookstore that sold newspapers and magazines from all around the world. When we couldn't find a parking space near the store, my role was to stay in the car so we wouldn't get a ticket! Other days, I went in with him and assisted him in choosing books and newspapers. He would go through the many papers, take out the pages he wanted to come back and read, and throw away the rest. If there was something good that he liked in a magazine, we were off to Kinko's or some other place where he could get loads of copies that he passed along to friends everywhere. He always had documents to back up what he was eager to discuss with you. Just when you had the audacity to think about an answer other than the one that he was going to offer, he could make you think you had done something wrong to even think what you were thinking!

You could ask him about anything. If anything was going on in the world, he would know about it and with just a few minutes to digest it, he could tell you all about it. The only other person I knew who could do that was the late Congressman Mervyn Dymally. I doubt that Greg ever met a vitamin that he didn't want to check out. Counting out his daily dose of vitamins was a major routine. He nor I ever took medicine because he always had a remedy for everything. The few times a doctor wrote a prescription, I just brought it home and put it away some place, because I already knew we'd be boiling onions, lemons, garlic, maple syrup and whatever else he had in his bag he thought should go in the tea! (Of course, he thought there was no such thing as a "not sweet" watermelon so long as you put a little maple syrup on it! I've tried it and he was right.)

Sometimes, the right ingredient to perfect the prescription for a cold or something else he recommended was a touch of bourbon and if we needed it on a Sunday that was a challenge because liquor stores in Washington, D.C. didn't sell liquor on Sundays. Once when I had a really bad cold, we found just a half pint of bourbon someplace after riding all over town to get it and since he had stopped drinking alcohol by then, we guarded that little half pint very carefully. Christian actually ultimately finished it off after his dad left us.

I never saw Greg at a loss for words. No matter what you asked him, he had an answer. After being around him for a while, I could answer many questions people asked him. I listened to him carefully. I read all of his books. I read his autobiography—the book called *Nigger*. Many people I know read it, but hesitated to say the name of the book. I read *Defining Moments in Black History: Reading Between the Lies.* There is so much history we need to know in that book. If you read nothing else by him, that is the one I would recommend. I read his book called *Dick Gregory's Natural Diet for Folks Who Eat.* I can't say I followed everything he said in the book, but I did my share. I read *Callus on My Soul: A Memoir.* I am still reading some of his other books and I am still learning what a wonderful world this would be if more people would allow themselves to get past the salty language he often used and tried to understand who he really was. We are seeing so much of what he warned us about, and we could have been ready for it when it happened.

After asking him a question, a few unlucky people made the mistake of asking him a question about what he had just said, then attempting to argue about what he said in response to the question. Wrong move! You were expected to listen without comment or question once you asked him something. When left alone to answer you, he was willing to talk non-stop until late at night or the wee hours of the morning. Once he was finished, you could expect him to fall asleep wherever he was.

He read so many newspapers, including foreign ones. He could easily point to the differences of opinion of the same event or act from around the world. He would also point out how people often gave two different responses depending upon their audience. It made no difference to him who his audience was; you always got the same response to the same question.

His daughter, Ayanna, is very talented. She did a show on Fathers' Day, June 17th, 2018. It was less than a year after her dad left us and as many times as I had seen her perform "Daughter of the Struggle" I found that performance very hard to watch. I thought about the first time her dad and I saw the first version of the show. As we sat there watching Ayanna's play, Greg teared up watching it. It was a very emotional experience for him. Later he commented that his friends Martin, Malcolm, and Medgar never had a chance to hear what their children said about them. He was feeling blessed that Ayanna had told such a powerful story about their family while he was still alive to hear it and we saw it so many more times. Each time something was added. Martin King, III watched the play with us once and called the play "magnificent and inspiring." It was definitely all of that and more.

CHAPTER 21

GREG'S THOUGHTS ABOUT BLACK WOMEN

Greg often talked about the power of the Black woman. In a joking manner, but in a serious way, he said, *"A Black woman is the only woman in the world who can cut a man's tires to the rim with a butter knife!"* He also said the two strongest forces in the nation are the Black church and the Black woman. He agreed with me that despite all of our hardships, discrimination, disrespect by *gangsta* rappers and others, Black women have shown the strength and the know-how to overcome whatever gets in our way. We jump through hoops and accomplish what we set out to do. No matter what, we are rarely afraid to take on challenges.

When white women received the right to vote with the support of Black women, some were okay with leaving us out. It took another forty plus years through dangerous conditions and numerous efforts for us to vote. We've pushed our way to victory for not only Black women, but for all women, including those who didn't offer to support our issues. When Black women were not in the race, so often it was necessary for us to vote for the lesser of two evils. We always did what we had to do. Our efforts are beginning to pay off, but some are trying to diminish our strength.

In this 2020 election, we played an important role in electing Black women in a larger number than ever and played an important role in the victories of others. President Joe Biden often recognizes the role we played in his election. Greg always applauded us for our unity and our willingness to do what was best for our community even when we were treated unfairly. His message always reminded us of the importance of being lovable.

A Black woman has often faced threats on her life for saying far less damaging things than the 45th president says daily, and until now he has gone unpunished. I've faced my share of threats for speaking truth, but I've never backed down from saying what I believed to be right. As we face the numerous threats to Black women, it's important for us to come to the defense of other Black women. I remember Greg's teachings about speaking up for others as I witness threats against Congresswoman Ilhan Omar, and I am compelled to speak out against those threats. A Trump supporter boldly threatened to "put a bullet" through Congresswoman Omar's skull. Greg would expect me to stand up for her and I do. I even invited her to be an honoree at our 2019 awards ceremony to let her know that someone admired what she was saying and doing. So many of her colleagues said nothing when she was being attacked.

We don't have to agree with everything she says or with what anybody says in order to defend their right to speak. If we don't stand with people like Congresswoman Omar and other Black women when they speak up on issues with which we might agree, but remain too afraid to say so, we should not be surprised that when they come in the morning, it could be for any one of us. It's tragic that so many for whom Black women have done so much leave negative and untrue words about Black women unchallenged. Greg never made lukewarm statements when the situation called for boldly speaking up. That is a lesson he ingrained in me. I could not call myself a Dick Gregory disciple while being too afraid to speak out on important issues.

Congresswoman Omar is our sister, and we must speak up for her rights. The system tries to crush her today, but it could be any one of us tomorrow. Those of us who understand are not afraid. Those of us who have been through similar treatment know how lonely it can be when even our friends are afraid to protect our rights. All I have to do when in doubt about getting involved is to remember the dangerous conditions under which Greg acted or spoke out and I know what I have to do.

What's happening with Ms. Omar is one more effort to silence Black women. Critics see the power we have when we work in unity. Twenty Black women mayors in Louisiana, including in the two largest cities, is an example of the power of Black women. We have Black women mayors in San Francisco, Washington, D.C., Baltimore, Rochester, Charlotte, Flint, Toledo, Boston, Atlanta, Chicago, St. Louis, and numerous smaller cities. I have met many as a member of the Board of Directors of the World Conference of Mayors and Historically Black Towns, but you get the point. We have a Black woman who ran strongly for President of the United States and is now Vice-President, Kamala Harris. We have many new Black women in Congress, joining a strong group already there.

Think about what Sojourner, Harriet, Ida B, Fannie Lou, Diane Nash, Ella Baker, Shirley Chisholm, and others went through to bring us to where we are today. Let's not lose the momentum by our silence that is interpreted as our consent when one of our sisters is attacked. Greg was always there for Black women who were trying to achieve something for our people. He always tried to make Black women feel good, to be proud of who we are. He would tell us that Egyptian queens were Black. Liz Taylor was simply playing in a movie when she portrayed Cleopatra.

As for his wife, Lil, Greg always spoke lovingly and highly of her. No matter where he went or to whom he was talking, he spoke respectfully of her. Occasionally, he talked about their beginning relationship and her getting pregnant before they were married. To that, he said he was taught that if you got a woman pregnant, you married her. So, once he learned of the pregnancy, they got married; and while he was not able to fully take care of her at that time, he took her to his family's place in St. Louis to live while he could grow in his profession and be able to better care for his family. Forever thereafter, he did that.

CHAPTER 22

LESSONS I LEARNED FROM GREG

1. No matter how much I wanted to get a word into a conversation, I learned to listen, and I did learn a lot. Wit and wisdom flowed from him like a river. He knew something about almost everything. To do that, he always had me reading something. He said that in order to learn, reading and listening were very important skills and that it was important to do more listening than talking.

2. In encouraging me to be strong when things required strength, he would tell me the story of the butterfly and the bald eagle. He said, *"Strong is not brawn. The delicate butterfly can fly all the way across the Atlantic Ocean, but the Bald Eagle can't make that flight."* In various aspects of my life, I've had to go against some of the seemingly strongest people, with far greater resources than I had, but with his advice and support I more often than not was successful. He taught me to believe in my own abilities without assuming the person I was up against had a stronger hand.

3. He would use the simplest of examples to make a point. He once said, *"If you want to see real power, get up early in the morn-*

*ing and watch the sun rise and smack darkness out of the sky, with-
out making a sound."* That was a lesson one hardly notices
about the simplest of acts that make a difference in our lives.
Now, every morning that I wake up, I rejoice at how the sun
miraculously rises, making everything look brighter than the
night before!

4. He knew everybody and everybody knew him. We could be
    walking down the street and often a brother would ask him
    for a dollar. If he had just one, he gave it to him. If he didn't
    have one, he would turn to me to borrow one. No matter how
    many times he did that, he never forgot to pay it back. It could
    be months later, but he never forgot. Since he's been gone, I
    find myself giving out more dollars than usual! His giving was
    a lesson in generosity.

5. Every time a new book came out on certain subjects, I was in
    for a late night of reading. He'd buy two of each book, bring
    them to my place and ask me to read to him until I had to prop
    my eyes open to finish the book some nights. He could be out
    of the country and when he needed a quote—no matter what
    time of night—he would call me to find the quote and read it
    to him. I learned a lot by reading for him.

6. He taught me about carrying Christ's Disciples with me at all
    times. He wasn't the kind of person who went to church every
    Sunday, but he was highly spiritual and could easily explain
    Biblical words and concepts.

7. He would say that Black people should never feel guilty about
    Black people voting for Black people because we Black people
    have been voting for white people all of our lives. He would
    say, *"It's time to learn to vote for our own. The white man's ice is no
    colder than ours!"* Unfortunately, no matter what you do, there

are still Black people who will vote against the masses of our people for their own self-interests. All you have to do is look at people who expressed their support for Donald Trump in the 2016 and 2020 elections.

8. Sometimes I would just want to wring my hands and ask why every Black person didn't see the need to get up and go out to vote in every election. His response to that was, *"Baby, the Black people who told you they're not voting in the upcoming election didn't vote in the last one and don't plan to vote in the next one."* That was a lesson in how much time to spend on somebody who argued against the need to vote in a certain election, so you would never be able to convince them otherwise.

9. He taught me patience because impatience is just another way to stress you out with no apparent good ending.

10. From him I learned that work for our causes never took a pause or a vacation, and just because it was a holiday or a weekend, didn't mean we could afford to have a free weekend, a vacation from everything or the ability to celebrate every holiday. There was always a rally for one cause or another and we made many of them at the expense of taking personal time.

CHAPTER 23

ACTIVISM THEN AND NOW

During a recent uprising in Wisconsin, I sat listening to the news coming out of Kenosha about two peaceful protesters being murdered by a white vigilante. I wondered how much more of this could go on with such casualness while white law enforcement and white politicians seal their lips. The night of the shooting, the young white man went about the street firing his gun. Not a word from the police on the scene that, no doubt, could have prevented the shooting of two people. They had to have seen him. He was carrying a long gun as he went into a volatile area. No one stopped to even question him. He then just walked past the police after the murders with his gun in hand and casually went back to his home in Illinois. No Black person could have gotten away with that or been released shortly thereafter.

On the other hand, I was watching Doc Rivers on the edge of tears, speaking as a father, asking, "Why do we keep loving this country and the country not loving us back? We need better. We must demand better..." I know Greg would have agreed.

LeBron James was so upset that he publicly used the word, f***. I'd never heard him go there before, but I could understand his agony. Athletes refused to play their games—both male and female. And I don't have to ask what Greg would have said. I am thinking about how he would have responded to the turmoil, and how proud he would have been of the athletes, entertainers, young people, some white people, and how they all responded to the shooting of Jacob Blake in Philadelphia and the two peaceful protesters in Kenosha. I'm thinking back to years ago when Colin Kaepernick took a knee against white supremacy. A few of his former teammates joined, but he paid a heavy price for protesting. Here we were again. It never seems to stop. If Greg were still with us, he would have been in Kenosha or Philadelphia with the protesters. He was never afraid to walk into the fire!

There were so many times, Greg would say, "It's over." He would say it in such a way that it was scary. I always wondered what he meant because he said it so convincingly, but he never really told me exactly what that meant. Since he's been gone, I now know the answer. The Black Lives Matter movement is showing us every day that things that once went unnoticed or forgotten in a few days will no longer work. What he meant was that casually treating white supremacy is over and will not be going back to *normal*. The January 6th, 2021 riots/revolts incited by Donald Trump further made us understand that business as usual in America is over, too. Even most white people would agree with that. Black people protest many evils in our society—and yes occasionally those protests result in violence—but that was not the reason for the protest. The violence often comes from outsiders who are intentionally disrupting the peaceful actions. On the other hand, we saw thousands of white people violently protesting when they went to the U.S. Capitol on January 6th, 2021 to destroy not only the Capitol, but also lives and attempts at destroying our democracy! Black people have never done that.

Because we spent so much time together, I don't have to ask what Greg would think about the response to all the killings and police shootings that have been going on for so long. In recent years, it seems to have been worse than usual. Ahmaud Arbery was killed by men playing cops. Breonna Taylor who was sleeping in her bed bothering no one, was killed by police. George Floyd was brutally killed by a policeman's knee on his neck until he lost consciousness and died. Rayshard Brooks, who just fell asleep in his car, was shot in the back by a policeman. Then came the seven shots to the back of Jacob Blake in front of his children and the officer shooting him didn't even get charged! Greg would be so impressed with all the Black men who have spoken out regarding these latest tragedies.

I listened to Shannon Sharpe (former football player, pro-football Hall of Famer and former analyst for CBS Sports), talk about Greg's solution to end police brutality. Greg said, "Give them something to lose. How do you make a cop change? It's simple. You pass legislation and say every cop has to be insured. Everybody carrying a gun has to be insured... (and say to the cop) 'The first time you violate that, you lose your license…Now, do you hate *niggas* more than you like feeding your family?' Give them something that they can't afford to lose…"

Greg would have been deeply touched by Doc Rivers' comments when he said, "How dare the GOP talk about fear when we're the ones getting killed!" He was emotional, rightfully, with obvious tears when he discussed the shooting of Jacob Blake in the back seven times! All you hear about is Donald Trump and all of them talking about fear. Doc Rivers was right when

he went on to say, "It's amazing why we keep loving this country and this country does not love us back." After the shooting of
Jacob Blake, women's basketball players in the WNBA wore black
tee-shirts that read "Arrest the Cops Who Killed Breonna Taylor."
They postponed scheduled games, saying they were reflecting
and recommitting to the social justice causes that underpin their
season. To date, no one has paid for taking Breonna's life.

Former NBA basketball star Chris Webber spoke eloquently
and was near tears when he said, "I'm here to speak for those
who've always been marginalized." We heard from athletes like
LeBron James and others. Some invoked the name of Colin
Kaepernick. I always kneel when I hear Colin's name, and I have
so much admiration for what he did to ultimately get so many
athletes involved in taking on important issues. Much of U.S.
sports came to a halt when Jacob Blake was shot in the back while
obviously posing no threat to anyone. We witnessed so many
actions, including walkouts from leagues such as the National
Basketball Association and Major League Baseball. This was
definitely historic. No matter what it cost, they took a stand for
racial justice. Greg could not have imagined athletes in such great
numbers coming out in unity against racism, but I know he would
have been pleased by so many who finally realized their responsibility and their power.

Greg detested hearing about making America great again. He
often said those who talk about making America great again act
like America was once great for all of us. I don't know what goes on
in heaven, but if he has gotten the word about these great athletes
rising up and taking charge of the conversation about racism, he
would just sit back and say, *"Maybe some of you heard what I meant
when I said, Wake Up and Stay Woke!"*

CHAPTER 24

HE NEVER LEFT

In early August of 2017, I had to go out of town and when I got back home, I didn't hear from him and he wasn't answering his telephone, nor had he called me while I was out of town. That was most unusual because I spoke with him many times nearly every day, so I was concerned. I kept calling him, but I kept getting no answer. I finally heard from one of his children who informed me he was at Sibley Hospital. I immediately dashed over to the hospital where his daughter Ayanna and I stayed with him until his son Greg came over to spend the night with him. The whole time I was there, I stood by his bedside while he held onto my hand. He was obviously in a lot of pain. For the rest of that week, I spent as much time as I could, holding his hand, and coaxing him to eat a little bit of food and drink some water.

I went home late on the Friday night, but came back Saturday morning at which time he'd already been taken for a walk outside the hospital. When he was brought back to his room, we watched the protests in Boston that were related to what had recently happened in Charlottesville, Virginia. There were many friends in the room. Some were pretty noisy. At a certain point, he said loudly, "Shut the f*** up. You need to wake up and stay woke so you can learn something. You can't learn anything by talking all the time." Everybody got quiet. Then, I made an effort to control traffic in his room to keep things quiet. The noise was obviously bothering him. Friends were stopping by. They were sending flowers. The flowers were all around the foot of his bed, but at a certain point, he wanted them moved from where they were all around him. I have no idea why, but he didn't want them in front of him. Ayanna and I quickly moved the plants and flowers and placed them on the floor as much out of his sight as we could. In addition to friends who were visiting, other friends were calling from around the country. Some who I remember calling that morning were Minister Louis Farrakhan, Coach Dale Brown from Louisiana State University, and Rev. Jesse Jackson.

Friends were pouring in all afternoon. It was as if they knew he was about to leave us. Again, I tried to control traffic in and out of the room by asking some people to wait in the hall while I urged some to leave the room so others could come in. The doctors informed us he would be able to go home Sunday—the next day. His son, Christian and others began making plans for him to go home by arranging a hospital bed, getting a physical therapist, etc. for his apartment. A couple of nurses came after I kept going to the desk to inform them he was in a lot of pain. They came and tried to give him blood, which he refused until he looked at me to okay what they were about to do. They tried, but he kept rejecting it until I told them to stop. By then, they had put the needle in both of his arms too many times. I was holding back tears because I knew how much he was hurting, and I knew what they were trying to do was not making him feel any better.

For a long time, I wondered if I had done the right thing by telling the nurses to stop.

Some of Greg's daughters had been arriving throughout the day. Lil and Paula came in the late afternoon on Saturday. After greeting them, a few of us left the room and went down to the lounge to allow the immediate family to be alone with him. About an hour later, several doctors came to his room and several of us were called back to Greg's room. We gathered around to hear what the doctors were saying.

Greg was very attentive as they said they had finally figured out what the problem was, but they would have to take him to George Washington Hospital. There they told him they would have to do surgery. We began packing up his things to move out of the room. Various family members took the flowers, plants and his personal effects. As family members were leaving, I, too, left to go home before going to the George Washington Hospital to wait out the surgery the doctors had mentioned he would be having there.

Greg was taken from the room to go downstairs. As we left Sibley Hospital, we had the intention of meeting him at George Washington Hospital. Christian went downstairs in the hospital with his dad, but Greg never made it to the transport vehicle. I had just gotten home when Greg, his son, called me to say, "Dad just made his transition." In shock, I called Chef who rushed over to pick me up and we rushed back to Sibley Hospital. What seemed like a very long time of waiting to be able to see Greg before he was taken away, the family went down to the hospital morgue where Greg was all by himself now. The friends were gone. The family, except Christian, had gone. Christian had told me to wait, and he would come to tell me when I could spend my last moments with his dad. He walked back to the hospital morgue with me. I walked in the room, sat by Greg's bed and had a long talk with him. It was a one-way conversation while I promised him that I would carry on the many things we had started together. When I finished, I was numb. I was still in a state of disbelief. I didn't want to leave him there, but I had to.

I was scheduled to do the message at church the next morning. Through my tears, I was determined to do it. My pastor told me I didn't have to do it because she could fill in for me. I assured her I could handle it and that I really wanted to. I didn't know how I could do it, but I knew I wanted to do it. As many "impossible" situations we had been through together, there was no way I would not at least try. Chef came to take me to the church on Sunday morning. Tears just kept getting in the way. I was all choked up, but I was determined. Chef stood in the back of the church and coached me through it by reminding me to breathe deeply. He was like an orchestra director helping me to breathe. I walked up to the podium, did as he said, told a Dick Gregory joke, and I was ready for the message that came to mind. I don't know how, but I made it through. My pastor said it was the best one I had ever done. I was drained when it was over. Chef brought me back home. Several neighbors were at my place with champagne and food. They made me lie down on the little bed that Greg always walked in, sat down on, and went immediately to sleep. I did the same thing. When I woke up my friends were still there.

On the Monday morning after he left us, I was invited to be on the Roland Martin show. The station sent a limousine for me that morning. If you have ever seen or been on Roland's show, you know that can be a challenge! He seems to relish in playing "gotcha games" or at least that is the way his interviews seemed to me. As a radio host, I always try to make my guests feel comfortable while talking with them. Different strokes for different folks! It seems that he is successful doing it the way he chooses, but it wasn't something I relished doing that day. I just knew I had to do it because people were hungry for any little bit of information about Greg. Fortunately, others were on the program, so I didn't have to do it all by myself.

For the next several days, I was in a daze. A friend, Sam Murphy, made tee shirts for me for a whole week with reminders of my friend. He made cups with Greg's picture. Friends called from all over the country. Some were just calling to find out if what they'd heard about Greg was true because most of them could not believe he had died. Most had assumed he would live forever. I made that assumption, too. Sidney Miller stopped by my place for several days thereafter. He seemed to be in a daze too, and lost without Greg. Barbara Sanders, Dr. Lezli Baskerville, Bernice Seals, and a few other friends were very attentive. I managed to eat the great food they had prepared, and we managed to eliminate a few bottles of champagne! All that everybody did was helpful, but I knew that my life would never be the same now that Gregory was no longer with us. I had lost so many good friends before him, and I had not healed from many of them. I'd lost best friends before and I was shaken, but managed a pretty good recovery. In recent years before Greg, friends I'd lost were Gwen Scott-Taylor, Grambling's legendary head football Coach Eddie Robinson, Dr. James Hines, Jr., Georgia Maryland, Rev. Bennie Thayer, and Congressman Mervyn Dymally, but I had a bit of warning most of them were transitioning. Most had been seriously ill for a while. Not so with Greg. He was about to be discharged the following day, or so we had been led to believe, but he never left the hospital alive.

I knew how much I would miss the late-night calls that came just to see how I was doing or to ask me to find a passage in a book for him. I knew how much I would miss the flowers that came for no special occasion, and the stacks of cards he gave for every occasion and often for no occasion. They were all so beautiful, so carefully selected, that I never threw any of them away. I still have them, and I read his messages of encouragement often. He never gave just one card. He gave several. I think he would just go to the store, look through all the cards and select all that said what he wanted to say, but mainly all that were beautiful where the picture without words had a message.

We wouldn't be able to go to Jenny's Restaurant anymore, where we had spent so much time working through so many challenges and had such great times. As soon as we were seated, he would order my favorite, a small bottle of champagne. He would order his bourbon and Coke. Jenny, the owner, would come over and we'd chat until our food came, at which time she would make her exit. Her staff always treated us like we were royalty. They'd give me a hug and ask if we wanted the usual. We almost always did. Sometimes they would comp us with a new dish they wanted us to try. Jenny's was the place we went when we were tired, when we were sad about something, or when we were celebrating something. Even if I wanted to go without him now, I couldn't go to Jenny's because the restaurant has been torn down and the wharf is such a different place now. I do much of my walking in the area now, but there is no sign of the restaurant we loved so much and in which we spent so much time.

He loved movies. Often, he'd see the same movie eight or ten times. He would take friends he thought should see them. He would go so many times to get every ounce of meaning out of the movie. The last film we saw together was *Black Panther*. That was one of those WOW movies and I went back to see it after he was gone. I took our mutual friend, Art Rocker, because I knew he would want Art to see the movie.

As the family was preparing for the funeral, I was asked to assist with a few things. I followed up on initial contacts with some that Ayanna, Christian, and I completed. I also made initial or follow up calls to others who I thought were friends to do something related to the funeral. Some of the contacts were just about attending the service. I made calls to people who shall remain nameless for assistance or just regarding attendance, and helped with arrangements for some to be present. Positive responses came from Carlos Campbell, Andy Shallal, Terrence Scott, Juanita Britton (Busy Bee), Glenn Ellis, Doctah B, Cicely Tyson (who did a beautiful tribute via video) and others. On the other hand, many people called me regarding arrangements and expressed their condolences, but that was it. Calls had come to me from people who had never met him but knew who he was, and were grieving that he had left us. They were in disbelief because they found it hard to fathom that Dick Gregory would ever die!

I had a house full of friends for days leading up to the funeral. As they began to leave, I felt so lost. He'd left some shoes at my place that he would put on after we went walking and came back with wet or muddy shoes. I stumbled around in them for days. I guess that was my way of promising friends who had the expectation that I would walk in his shoes now that he was gone. I still get messages and photos that people think I would like to have. So many still tell me Dick Gregory stories about how they came to know him, and what they remember about him. Recently, a woman told me about his always having advice on what to take when you explained your problem. In her case, she was coughing violently. She said he told her to take a nasty tasting black cough drop but she couldn't think of the name of it. I immediately told her it must have been Olbas. She confirmed that is what it was. I knew that because I had heard him tell many people to do it! That included me.

I will always appreciate him for making me more flexible and adaptable. He taught me never to sit around and moan and groan about disappointments (and I have had a few), but to get up quickly, get back in the game, and never brood from losses or when you've been knocked down. I have sometimes made decisions that were not always in my best interest, but he taught me to take responsibility for the mistakes and work my way through them. I recognize that my challenges have been great, but he taught me to recognize that my blessings have been greater— and they have. He taught me to believe in rainbows, to be an "overcomer," and never give up when things are a bit rough. Most of my best friends and family members have never known many of my struggles along the way. Life still is a mixture of good and bad, but he taught me through example about getting up when life knocks you down—and I do that. That is one of the greatest lessons I learned from him, and I have come to believe I have not yet done everything God wants me to do.

Sometimes I think I am overly tolerant, but I believe being so saves me a lot of stress and grief. I recover from hurt quickly because I really work at it. I try not to sit around and moan and groan about disappointments. There's always something in front of me that requires me to get up and get back in the race.

Since Greg's been gone, I have decided to take more time to nurture my relationships and accelerate my spiritual growth with many of the tools I learned from him. I'm learning to recover from hurt more quickly—to really work at it and not feel guilty if I am not working every minute of the day. There's always something in front of activists that requires us to keep saying yes to every challenge, but since I have become more chronologically advanced, I have come to believe that even activists have the right to be free sometime—to take time to enjoy life! Greg certainly knew how to do that. I miss him so much, and I have had to learn to live with so many challenges alone since he's been gone. He could always make the seemingly worst challenge a *piece of cake!* He could always lead you to an answer for every question, a resolution for every challenge.

In all that he did, his wish was always to make people around him lovable and happy, and to make America live up to her promises for all of us. I still consider myself one of his students. He was the greatest mentor I could ever hope for. He has been called, "… one of the greatest Americans of modern times." I call him my best friend and one of the greatest friends of all time to so many! All of his messages are so relevant to me as we are going through some troubling times right now. I know he would have come up with some kind of solution for this coronavirus!

Most nights I get very little sleep because I feel compelled to find answers for people who have asked me to help them with something. No matter how I try, I rarely get to bed before one or two in the morning. Weekends and holidays are never a deterrent to working for one cause or reason or another. Being tired or sleepy never excuses finishing an important job. Many nights, I go to bed not knowing how I will make it the next day because the pressure to do something to help somebody, somewhere with something is so overwhelming that I keep pushing myself. When daylight comes, somehow, I remember Greg's words "Wake Up and Stay Woke." I try to do that every day. I get up and begin working on something that at least has the potential to help somebody.

CELEBRATION OF HIS LIFE

Greg wasn't buried right away. That came a few weeks later. It was a month later, to be exact, before the funeral and burial. That month was pure agony. During that time, I spoke with hundreds of people. Many later came to the funeral, called a celebration of life, that was held in Landover, Maryland at City of Praise Family Ministries, a major church that could hold thousands, and it did that day. There would have been more, but there was confusion about whether people needed a ticket to get into the church. They did not, but that word had gotten out and it kept some people from coming. The service was held September 19th, 2017. He had passed away exactly one month prior to the service on August 19th, 2017. The service was truly a celebration of his life. Even though it was off the beaten path and some had to park far away in order to get there, they came to pay their last respects.

Among the attendees were Bishop William Barber, who was a speaker, Minister Louis Farrakhan, another speaker, and Bill Cosby who was having his legal battles at that time, but people applauded him for being there. Others present were my good friend President of NAFEO, Dr. Lezli Baskerville and MSNBC talk show host Lawrence O'Donnell, who stayed the whole time and didn't just walk through and leave, like many white people often do.

There were many well-known natural health gurus like Doctah B who came from Atlanta. Ed Weinberger (screenwriter and producer who was a very close friend) came from California.

I thought Ed was treated badly on the program by the moderators who obviously didn't have a clue who he was and what he meant to Greg. On the other hand, they allowed Congresswoman Maxine Waters to use the time of at least ten scheduled speakers, pushing the program into very late at night, but they rudely pulled Ed and others off the stage in just a few minutes. I didn't get any better treatment! Maybe I got two minutes before I was ushered off as if I had gone overtime. I was not happy because I had practiced my three minutes of what I was to say, and I knew I would not be going over the time I was given. I am a professional speaker and I know how to stay within my time limit. I am a great respecter of time. It was humiliating and hurtful to be treated otherwise.

Many people called later to express their dismay that I was treated so rudely. Those of us who were doing what we were told to do were cut even shorter to allow Maxine to speak as long as she chose to. Their allowing her to disregard the rules we had been given prolonged the time before the main speakers came on. Some people began leaving as she continued to talk long past her time limit. Cicely Tyson had opened the program with a beautiful video. She was receiving an award in Hollywood the same day of the funeral so she could not be with us in person as much as she wanted to be. Her video made it seem that she was there in person. Her message received heavy applause. But for Greg introducing us, I might never have known her personally. Her friendship was indeed precious.

By the time the program finally ended, I skipped the dinner/reception afterwards and went home. My house was filled with friends who had come from all across the country to be there for the celebration. I had to find a lot of sheets and pillows during that time. One woman I had never met actually called me from California and made it sound like I had no choice but to allow her to stay at my home because of all the *great things* she said Greg had told her about me, and that he had told her if she ever needed anything to call me! She did just that. One of the things she needed was a place to stay. She arrived from the airport in a taxi for which she had no money to pay! The taxi driver summoned the police, so I wound up having to rescue someone I didn't even know. Before leaving, she did return my money, but how does one travel all the way across the country without taxi fare?

On the same day that Greg was buried, news came that his sister had died. The day following the celebration at the church, Nick Cannon came to be with the family at the hotel where some were staying for the funeral. Killer Mike came, and so did others, too many to remember who they were. On the Sunday morning, we had a program near the Howard Theater where I was a speaker, then we had a procession through several streets, with music and many people following the casket to Ben's Chili Bowl where Greg's picture had recently been painted on the side of the building. I had presented him for the occasion. Yet, there were those who were conspicuously absent. There was nothing I could do about it, but I did take names! It was glaring who was not there and gave no explanation. I won't judge their reasons, but among them were people who had relied on him for favor after favor through the years to bring life to their conventions and programs. Greg always obliged them. No matter how much money they made when his presence packed their events, most never gave him a dime.

Christian and I have gone back to the burial site many times for his dad's birthday and for other occasions that were meaningful to Greg. It's still hard for me to see him in a casket pushed into a wall that carries his name. He was a free spirit, and it doesn't seem right to have him locked up like that. I used to leave him notes when I visited him and when I came back, the notes would be gone. I told myself he came out and picked them up! Most likely, it was the clean-up crew that took them away!

I still often shed tears as I think about Greg, and it is at those times, I remember what true friendship is—and that he's still guiding my work in many ways. I try to make myself understand that when he left us, a yoke was lifted from him and that he is in a better place where he has no more pain. Lord knows he experienced enough pain that last week of his life. I miss him every day, and I am proud of him and all the good he did for so many when he was here with us. At those times, I remember 2nd Timothy 4-7 and I can truly say, "He fought a good fight (all of his life). He finished his course. He kept the faith." His memory will always be with me, and I am blessed for having known him and still call him my best friend, my running buddy who ran an awesome race.

Last photo taken together of Dick Gregory and Dr. E. Faye Williams, Esq.

DICK GREGORY'S WEIGHT LOSS SYSTEM

HERBS

Burdock	3 capsules in the morning, 3 in the evening
Buchu	3 capsules in the morning, 3 in the evening
Dandelion	3 capsules in the morning, 3 in the evening
Uva Ursi	3 capsules in the morning, 3 in the evening
Juniper Berries	3 capsules in the morning, 3 in the evening
Golden Seal	1 cup in the morning, 2 cups in the evening
Comfy (Tea)	2 cups in the morning, 2 cups in the evening (sweeten with maple syrup)
Herbal Laxative	2 capsules in the morning, 2 in the evening

VITAMINS AND SUPPLEMENTS

Zinc	1 capsule in the morning, 1 in the evening
Evening Primrose Oil	1 capsule in the morning, 6 in the evening
Vitamin B6 (500 mg)	1 capsule in the morning, 1 in the evening
Vitamin B2	1 capsule in the morning, 1 in the evening
Vitamin B12	1 capsule in the morning, 1 in the evening
Vitamin C	3 capsules in the morning, 3 in the evening (2000 mg time-released)
Vitamin E (400 I.U.)	1 capsule in the morning, 1 in the evening
Enzyme CoQ10	2 capsules in the morning, 2 in the evening

MENU

Breakfast: Nothing but fruit before 12:00 noon.

Lunch: Eat all raw vegetable salad or just fruit.

Dinner: Cook 1/2 cup of rice (brown or white). While rice is cooking, mix the following in a blender: 1/2 onion, 4 pieces of garlic, 9 tbsp. olive oil, 6 tbsp. Braggs Liquid Amino Acids. After blending, pour mixture in a saucepan. Heat, then pour over the rice once it is cooked.

Water: Always drink a minimum of eight (8) glasses of spring water each day.

Beverage: Squeeze the juice from 8 lemons, 4 oranges and 2 grape-fruits. Mix with 1 1/2 cups of pure maple syrup in a one-gallon container. Fill up with spring water.

APPENDIX

Dick Gregory's Caribbean Shake for Optimal Health (formerly The Bahamian Diet).

- **A unique whole food based dietary supplement** formulated to promote a normal immune system with 59 highly digestible ingredients chosen to support optimal health, nourish your body, support healthy brain activity and cognitive function to enhance overall health.
- **Dick Gregory's 4X based, 100% vegan, gluten free, plant based protein powder** will help satisfy your appetite and support healthy intestinal micro flora.
- **Supports insulin levels** already in normal range. Designed to help satisfy cravings and increase energy to help you regain and maintain control of your health and support immunity.
- **Workout recovery:** May reduce fatigue and increase vigor during strenuous exercise. Promotes the increase of lean body mass. Helps maintain a healthy weight by promoting normal fat metabolism.
- **Superior taste** and **health promoting** botanicals. Dick Gregory's Caribbean Shake is Non-GMO, Allergen friendly and Cholesterol Free. Does not contain Artificial Flavors, Sweeteners, or Colors, Dairy products, MSG or Soy. NOTE: Settling may occur. Containers are filled by weight; each container supplies 15 servings.

http://bit.ly/caribbeanshake

Nancy Pelosi
Democratic Leader

February 6, 2015

Mr. Dick Gregory
c/o Dr. E. Faye Williams
National Congress of Black Women, Inc.
1250 Fourth Street, Southwest, Suite WG-1
Washington, D.C. 20024

Dear Mr. Gregory:

Congratulations on receiving your Star on the Hollywood Walk of Fame on February 2nd! This honor is truly well-deserved.

As a comedian, you have made people laugh and brought joy into the lives of so many. As a civil rights activist, you have made so many open their hearts and minds, building a better nation for all of us. Your storied and inspiring career changed the face of comedy across our nation and around the world. You are an inspiration to us all, and your legacy will be remembered for generations to come.

Congratulations again, Dick! Thank you for your outstanding leadership, longtime friendship, and support. Paul and I send our best wishes to you, Lillian, and your beautiful family.

best regards,

Nancy Pelosi

NANCY PELOSI
Democratic Leader

For Speaking Engagements, Book Signings,
Appearances, and Interviews...

CONTACT

Dr. E. Faye Williams, Esq.
1250 4th Street SW, WG1
Washington, D.C. 20024

📞 (202) 554-0159
✉️ drefayewilliams@gmail.com
🧭 www.dickgregorysociety.org
𝕏 @DrEFayeWilliams
📷 @dickgregorysociety
💼 linkedin.com/company/the-dick-gregory-society

Made in the USA
Las Vegas, NV
01 May 2021

22321735R00125